*For Megan, Matthew, Hannah and Anne*

# Stand-up Marketing

John McRae

To Rachel,

With Very Best Wishes,

*[signature]*

# Stand-up Marketing ®

# John McRae

© 2012, John McRae

Self-publishing, first published in Great Britain in 2012

ISBN 978-0-9573872-0-1

john@standupmarketing.com

www.standupmarketing.com

# Contents

# THE WARM-UP ACT

*About this book and the 'comedian' who has taken your money!*

Hi, my name is John McRae and I simply **have** to introduce myself to you.

That first sentence of this book will become increasingly relevant as you make your way through it. For now I would just say that I have in 25 years, completed some 2,000 marketing projects across every marketplace imaginable. During that time I have seen it all - the good, the bad and the downright hilarious!

Although I have worked with many large UK and international, commercial and non-commercial organisations, for me the thrill of working with new start-up enterprises is unrivalled.

Their drive and passion are thrilling to witness. Most start their own business, not so they can drive around in a Roller, or count their millions, but because they want to live their dream and help benefit their families in the process.

Of course by successfully doing that, they also benefit the economy through taxes and employment - so success for them gives a genuine win-win situation.

Tragically however, around 50% never make it to year three and while successful marketing alone can't prevent every casualty, it really can go a very long way to increasing the odds in their favour.

When I decided to write a marketing book that was my mission; however there was a problem.

Three years ago I conducted research with a number of small businesses the majority of who said they had never read a book on marketing nor completed any kind of course.

Many admitted that they didn't **really** understand marketing, but just found books on the subject boring and not relevant. Some said they found it impossible to relate their small business, as a plumber, caterer, hairdresser and the like, to international giants such as Microsoft.

I began then to develop a new approach, that of offering practical tips and advice to start-ups, from the many other small business clients with whom I've worked over the years.

It worked. The new companies realised they could shorten their own learning curve (and pain) by seeing how those who had previously been in the **same** situation as themselves had handled it. Even when the outcome of the example was not successful, this too was valuable, potentially preventing them from making the same mistakes.

This is one of the main elements of the book, real problems and real solutions, experienced by other small companies. Those who are featured in this book have freely allowed part of their story to be told, hoping that in some way it will help others reading it - and that for me is a display of the very best in people and I salute each of them for their generosity of time and goodwill.

If practical experiences, advice and shortcuts from other small businesses make up one key element of this book, then **humour** is the other!

My best friend Arnaud de Beaumont has told me many times that one of the best ways of keeping people interested is to 'make them smile'. So following his advice I added humour and trialled the new mix in my marketing lectures to small businesses.

The combination proved a powerful one with many times more feedback from those attending the lectures and workshops than ever before.

I even began to be introduced as '*Mr Stand-up Marketing*' and so the concept gained a *brand* and an identity, which in turn became the title for this book.

Zany photos twinned with unusual chapter headings may be foreign to other books on the subject of marketing, but as long as they help you stay with it to the end, they will have done their job, as I believe your new business's chances of survival and growth will be greatly increased by finishing it.

This book is not so much about the myriad of ways to spend your money on promoting your product or service, but more about **you, your** offering, **your** position in the market, **your** customers and how to better connect with them.

Getting this straight will mean that every penny you then spend on communicating will be accurately spent, maximising your chances of a profitable return.

You have already bought this book (if not put it back on the shelf **now!**), and in doing so have taken an important step in the right direction, now take another... **read it!**

## 1.1 Avoid an empty theatre…
### …it's better playing to a full house

On the Home page of my website (www.standupmarketing.com) there is a video that begins with me playing the role of a stand-up comedian being introduced on stage.

I come on bubbling with excitement, announcing enthusiastically, "Hello ladies and gentlemen, boy do I have a show for you! I've been working on this for months and I know you are going to love it, it's going to be…"

At this point my voice trails away to silence and the camera swings round to reveal a completely *empty* auditorium. No audience.

Starting a new business can often be like that; you have an idea, work hard on it for months, investing your time, energy and money, only to find that on the day you launch no one turns up. **No customers.**

From that moment you find yourself playing catch-up, trying to spread the word and drum up interest. The problem is that this often involves ploughing even further resources into something that might just not be of sufficient interest to consumers. It's a little like a golfer who goes to the practice ground himself and hits golf balls for two hours and then wonders why he isn't getting any better when he plays on the course. It's because he has been practising the wrong things - and ironically actually becoming better at doing them wrong!

If it isn't right in the first place, you need to stop and review.

That is why I urge all my new clients to begin as early as possible the process of working through your offering to the market; what does it **really** have that current offerings don't, who will these unique properties benefit and how best to then reach them.

Of course it is ideally better to do this *before* launching your enterprise, but even if you are already in business much can be done to sharpen your offering and message, thereby encouraging more customers, sales and profit.

When you launch your business it *is* show time and your business card, website and literature are like having your name up in lights - it's an exhilarating feeling, matched only by winning your first customer or sale.

So when it's time for 'curtain up' and for you to reveal what you have been working on behind the scenes, just make sure **your** target audience turn up.

The aim of this book is to help make sure that you not only have an audience, but critically the **right** one, one that will connect with your product or service - and pay you for it!

By being prepared and then performing well, you will gain their appreciation; enjoy many 'encores' **and** next time they will bring their friends with them.

## 1.2 "Didn't understand a word of that...
   ...*we'd better hire him!"*

So there I was, somewhat bizarrely sitting in an audience of business people, at of all things a seminar on **marketing!** It had been arranged for the region's small businesses by the Chamber of Commerce and as I'd been booked as a speaker for a future event I thought I'd sit in so I could see what ground this lecturer was covering.

After what became one of the longest hours in my life, I began to realise that despite being in the marketing business I had absolutely no idea what the speaker was talking about and by the time we were on the sixth graph of *'Marketing in a global economy'* I no longer cared.

He covered everything from the '3 Ds' to the '7 Ps' of marketing and to be honest I could have tossed a few F's in as well by the time he'd finished.

In fact the thing I remember most about his talk, was right at the end. I was sitting next to two businessmen, who like the rest of the audience had come along to learn how marketing could help put their small enterprise on the map. As the speaker finished, one turned to the other and said, "I didn't understand a word of that, we'd better hire him."

I couldn't believe it! Firstly the speaker had failed to connect with his audience, whose businesses were a million miles removed from *'global economies'* and now he had so bewildered them that he was going to profit by it! *Amazing!*

It also summed up everything that leaves me cold about sections of the marketing industry - we just love to make things complicated! Why? Because then you need to hire us to explain it all - **genius!**

Another good example of this was when I went to meet the owner of a small business. I began by asking her what her understanding of marketing was. She admitted very little and said that she found the subject too theoretical, hard to grasp and therefore almost impossible to *apply* successfully to her small enterprise.

She explained that before starting the business she had purchased a book on marketing, one that proclaimed to cover 'the principles' which she felt would be sufficient for her needs.

"So how did you get on with it?" I enquired, suspecting I knew what the answer would be.

"Well I almost made it to the end of the second chapter," she admitted. Then sounding a note of triumph, she added, "However it did eventually come in handy - it's behind you, I use it to prop the door of this office open when it gets a little stuffy!"

Sure enough when I turned round there in all its glory, or not, was the marketing book serving a small business owner, but **never** in the way its author had intended.

Seeing the irony in the situation I actually offered to purchase the book from her there and then for the full cover price. She thought I was completely mad, but like any good business person she pocketed the money anyway (no receipt!) before I could change my mind.

Then in an instant she replaced the marketing book's 'supporting' role with another from the shelf, this time *'Accountancy for beginners'*. So maybe it's not just marketing books that business people don't read!

There is nothing more frustrating though than trying to understand something that you have an interest in, but then giving up because you can't fully grasp it.

I recently listened to a professor who was guesting on a radio programme explaining with great excitement that experiments by Cern scientists at the Large Hadron Collider had seen a level of certainty in their data that enabled them to claim the discovery of a new particle consistent with the Higgs boson.

The professor was asked by the programme presenter to explain more about what they had found so the listeners could better understand the significance.

The professor said the team's data had corresponded to a particle weighing in at 125.3 gigaelectronvolts (GeV) - about 133 times heavier than the protons that lie at the heart of every atom. He added that they had attained a confidence level just at the 'five-sigma' point - about a one-in-3.5 million chance that the signal they see would appear if there were no Higgs particle.

There was a pause in the studio broken by the programme's presenter saying he had just received a one word text from a listener that simply read, "**What?**"

And therein lies the problem; if people can't fully understand something, no matter how much they want to, they will never fully appreciate the value of it.

So I want to make a personal invitation to you now and perhaps an unusual one for an author. If there is **anything** in this book that you *don't* *'understand a word of'*, email me and I will be pleased to try and better explain it to you.

It's not just important that you understand the contents of this book, it could be **vital** to your company that you do, so please if something is unclear don't hesitate to ask.

## 1.3  This book needs *you!*
### Test your business model here…

This book is about **you** and **your** business no one else!

In it I will often refer to your business as 'you' or 'your offering' – because as a new company you **are** your business

So at every stage I would like you to imagine that I am actually sitting with you and no one else is present - just you and me. Every word I 'speak' is to you, every question I ask, every challenge I issue, everything is aimed exclusively at **you** and **your** business.

So for example whenever I relate a case history from another business; turn it back on your own situation and see if it could be used to your advantage.

Test your business model against each section and the examples of how others have done things, does it stand up, or does it need re-evaluating?

Of course some readers of this book will not be a start-up enterprise. While still a small business some may have become established and are now looking to move up to the next level. So if that is you, the next few paragraphs are aimed in your direction.

Before accepting any new client I always insist in having a 'get to know you' session, so that I can begin to understand the heartbeat of their operation. The truth is I do this so that the owners can more fully understand their **own** business and its direction. By looking at their business through different eyes they are often confronted with issues, negative and positive, which they had never before properly addressed.

In such an exercise I ask them many questions, so that together we can understand what makes them tick, and what they want from a marketing project.

This may sound a bit of a wasted exercise, as everyone says they want more customers, more sales and more profit. Yet within this there are many variances that need to be taken into account when formulating a game plan. An example of this was when I visited a partnership of two years standing who felt that they were making progress but could do so much more.

To begin with their answers to my questions dovetailed perfectly, they were in complete accord with regard to wishing to achieve more sales with higher margins. However when I asked if they saw this through increased turnover within their existing customer base or from new clients, there was a pause, before one plumped for new customers and the other for fresh business.

The one who wanted growth from existing customers argued that they were already set up to service them and so seeking ways to increase their sales levels would be easier and less costly. The other retorted that the danger they would then be in was that all their business eggs would be in just a few baskets.

While both made valid points, the problem was that if they wanted to proceed with *both* avenues they needed not one but two strategies, with the associated costs and time commitment that would bring.

Following a few minutes debate on the merit of each direction I then asked another question, "Are you also looking for an exit strategy at some point in the future and if so when?" In other words would they consider selling their company in the future; if so were they thinking of doing so in the short, medium or long term? One of the partners immediately replied that he would consider building to sell in another two to three years, which was clearly news to the other who was looking to a much longer term.

I asked the question as it can make a difference to the way they promote themselves and to whom. The problem was, as they hadn't really worked out what they wanted to do and when, it made moving forward more difficult.

So if you are already an established business, before reading on think about what you'd like to achieve and when, given your current standing. Then as I examine different aspects of marketing, you can more appropriately decide if they are of interest for your business or not.

If for example your marketplace is becoming more crowded with competitors and you feel your offering needs greater clarity, then the 'why you' section of this book is a must, especially the chapter (7.0) 'A couple of mangoes and a load of bollards!'

Or it may be that you need a greater profit margin; if so the *'Say it with flowers'* case study (8.3) may provide food for thought.

Maybe you feel that you are not getting the level of consumer response that your product or service merits; then see the section on *'The Lost Ramblers'* (11.2).

Back to those of you who are just starting; if you feel confused by what marketing actually means in relation to your start-up business, read chapter 3.0, the delicately titled, *'What the \*%!@ IS marketing?'*

Better still, follow the formula right through from beginning to end, stopping to scribble notes on any point you think might work for your business - you will be surprised just how many notes you will end up with!

Then sort these into categories, prioritising them with target timelines as well as who in the company will be responsible for developing them. This will be your very own marketing strategy, all without having to employ my services - go on make me **unemployed!**

By getting your thinking clear **before** you spend any money on advertising, websites, literature, social media and the other items from today's ever growing menu of communications, it will maximise your chances of a profitable return when the time comes to invest.

# CHAPTER 2

# READY, AIM, FIRE!
# (NOT: READY, FIRE... **AIM!**)

*Starting a new business? Don't rush it!*

Whenever I meet a new business start-up I just love the energy and excitement they generate. Their **idea** is about to become their **business!** And of course they just can't wait to get started, can't wait to **tell** people.

While that is completely understandable, there is a danger which I would liken to the archery competition I watched at the London Olympics.

Apart from childhood memories of Robin Hood on the telly, this was the first time I'd actually studied the sport.

Unsurprisingly with gold, silver and bronze medals at stake, the archers didn't just walk up and let fly with their arrows, but instead each went through a meticulous preparation. This involved first checking their equipment, then their body posture and stance.

Next they considered the target and its position, together with any prevailing conditions which would have to be factored in, such as cross winds, before calculating the required trajectory for the arrow to fly.

Then and only then, after this detailed checklist was complete, did they release their arrow; for they knew that doing so after such preparation gave them the best chance of hitting the target.

After all should they miss, through cutting short their preparation, they could hardly go and ask for their arrow back to have another go!

Marketing **your** new business is like this. First you have to get *ready* for the marketplace with your offering. You have to make sure that your preparation is right and that you are clear and happy with your product or service and its direction.

This involves considering who and where your *target audience* are, in other words the people that you are counting on to buy your offering in sufficient numbers to keep you in business. What is it you've got that will hit the target with them?

Once the *ready* and *aim* preparations are complete and only when they are complete, you *fire* your *communication arrows*.

By this I mean select from the communications menu the most appropriate methods for *hitting* your target audience; such as: sales literature, website, social media, PR, advertising, trade or consumer directories, direct mail, or exhibitions.

The point is that you are now fully into the **Fire** phase and as such you will be **spending your money**; remember, *communications* = cost!

Therefore just as on the archery range it is important to get your preparations right **before** releasing your communication arrows; otherwise a result of *'Ready, Fire… AIM!'* may occur, causing you to have spent your money and completely missed the target.

Just like if you miss in archery, you can hardly go back to where you have spent your communications money and ask for it back, so you can *'have another go.'*

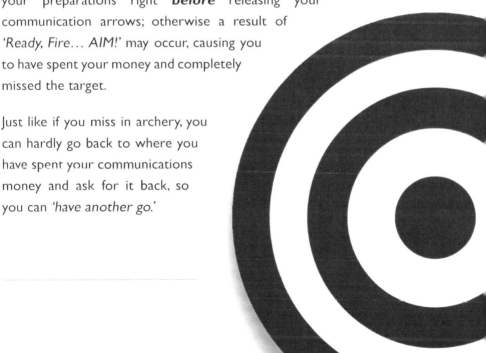

This sounds obvious doesn't it? And it IS obvious, yet time and again I meet businesses that do not spend enough time in preparation, but instead rush to communicate.

Therefore the purpose of this book is to help get your thinking straight about the *ready, aim* parts of your business, so when you do fire your communication arrows they are much more likely to hit their *target...* **your customers!**

NOTE: If you think the photograph at the beginning of this Chapter is bad, **believe** me it was the better of two evils when compared to me dressed as Robin Hood in green tights!

# CHAPTER 3

# WHAT THE *%!@ IS MARKETING?

*25 years and 2000 marketing projects summed up in just 30 seconds*

Some time ago I went to a business safari dinner, where you are paired with one other person for each course; a bit like speed dating but without the good bit at the end.

For the aperitif I was partnered with a lovely lady who ran a singing telegram and strip-o-gram business. I was somewhat hesitant to exchange cards for fear of later being apprehended, cuffed and strip-searched by a busty 'police lady' (although on reflection I may have been too hasty in that judgement).

Looking at my business card she said apologetically, "Marketing? I've just had some leaflets printed; otherwise I could have got you to quote for them." I shrugged and mumbled something like, 'Next time maybe?" I then listened as she described her latest business 'acquisition' - a singing caveman!

Over the carrot and coriander soup I joined the company of another lady, a successful business woman whose enterprise involved fitting and supplying bras. She was very interesting, although for once I found it difficult to go through my normal in-depth business diagnostic.

When I did however mention 'marketing' she replied, "Oh, I had a branding revamp last year." I couldn't help but smile at her use of the word '**bra**nding', but as she didn't, I guessed it wasn't meant to be funny and so returned to my soup.

I moved on to the main course, which I can only describe as, *trial by goujons of lemon sole.*

My companion was 'in insurance' and for the next 30 minutes I was reminded of a film I'd seen many years before, where a man was sentenced to be locked in a room for three days… *with an insurance salesman!*

I did at one point succeed in breaking into his sales spiel, blurting out, "Did I mention that I'm in marketing?"

There was a momentary pause before he replied, "I've got all the *market research* I need thanks very much," before continuing to berate me for having my professional and indemnity policies with two different companies.

Sweet, consisted of trifle (I *love* trifle!) and a director of an engineering company, who was less than complimentary towards the word *marketing*, summing up the entire profession as, "PR spin merchants," then belatedly adding, "Well I'm not **saying you**." But he was **thinking me!**

Somehow his verbal onslaught dissuaded me from mentioning to him the fact that some of his trifle and cream had fallen onto his tie and was slowly, but purposefully, making its way south to his trousers - **justice!**

I decided to cut my losses and skipping the coffee and mint creams, headed home. On the way I did think however that out of the four people I'd met, all of whom were in business, each had a different interpretation of what marketing actually was.

The first had thought it was connected with literature, the second believed it was to do with one's corporate identity, the third immediately referred to it as 'market research', while the last was convinced it was PR (Public Relations), the issuing of media releases to obtain 'free' and favourable publicity - or 'spin' as he put it.

It is hard to make something work for you if you don't really understand what it is, or as my friend Barbara used to say about marketing, "It's like trying to nail a jelly to a wall".

Well the good news is that in the next section I will prove to you that you **already understand** all you need to know about marketing!

*Now there's a disappointment since you've just bought the book!*

## 3.1 Marketing; all you need to know...
### ...in just 30 seconds

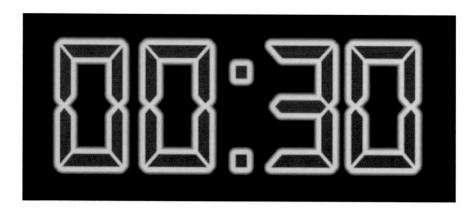

As you can see from the title of this section, I will now explain why in my opinion all you really need to know about marketing can be explained in the following exercise of just 30 seconds - or **less** if you read quickly!

I've presented this exercise on many occasions, from universities to business conferences. When I tell the audience that I'm about to encompass all the key elements of marketing in just 30 seconds, people appear to be genuinely impressed. They even regard me as they would a magician before he performs a seemingly impossible trick.

However as soon as I finish it virtually everyone is **disappointed** (that's showbiz for you!). Maybe **you** will be different?

First let me set the scene as this exercise requires a little bit of mind role-play on both our parts. I'd like you please to play the role of the sales manager of a car showroom, your responsibility is to maximise the sales of a particular car.

But not just **any** car! You are responsible for increasing sales of **Rolls Royce** cars.

My role in this exercise is that of a salesman who is visiting your showroom in an attempt to convince you that I have a product that if offered as a give-away with Rolls Royce cars will help increase their sales!

Once I have made my 30 second presentation to you, please let me know if I have a sale or not; deal or no deal!

So with the thought that you run a showroom for Rolls Royce cars let's begin (by the way I'm getting into character now as the salesman, in case you think I've completely lost the plot). Here we go!

*Hello and thank you for agreeing to see me today in your beautiful showroom and giving me the opportunity to show you a product that I believe will greatly help you to sell **more** Rolls Royce cars.*

*And the product I am offering you… the product that I know will increase sales… is… (I wish books could do a drum roll)…is…*

... pink furry dice!

*What do you think, do I have a sale?*

*No?*

*Well I could do them in blue? Green?*

*You're not buying this are you?*

*Good!* (THE END)

And that dear reader is **all** *you need to know about marketing in just 30 seconds*, thank you!

Don't tell me... you're disappointed, right? Well let's run the exercise one more time, only this time with a little more explanation.

To begin with the product I asked you to imagine you were representing, Rolls Royce is one of the most famous in the world. So the chances are your mind considered images of: glamour, exclusivity, prestige, heritage, luxury, quality... and of course, **price!**

You immediately knew that this was one of the more expensive cars in the world and so positioned it at the top end of the car market - high quality, high price.

You then immediately began to envisage the type of people who would be potential customers for that car. Even though you may not actually know any Rolls Royce owners, you felt confident enough to picture them in your mind, their probable likes and dislikes based on the product and the price.

So when I then introduced the somewhat tacky pink furry dice you didn't just **think** about Rolls Royce customers, you actually **became** one and saw the offering through **their** eyes and immediately the very thought jarred horribly!

There was **no** connection, **no** sale!

For me that exercise IS marketing. Whatever marketplace you go into, whether you have a product or a service, you will have to decide at which end of the marketplace it is going to sit. Will it be at the very top and be a luxury or superior performance offering, or perhaps at the opposite end of the market and be much more based on low price than quality.

Pink furry dice and a 'Roller' may well be an extreme example of how to fail to make a successful connection but it is an important way to understand marketing. Here's the summary in point format:

• The word 'marketing' comes from the 'market'. So begin by deciding what your product or service's **position** in your chosen market will be and then consider what occupying this means.

• Next, based on this market position, identify who your optimum **target audience** is for your offering.

• Now **really get to know** your target audience, their likes, dislikes, their buying habits, key words they use, places they visit, publications they read and so on, until you have a very clear picture of them.

- Then before firing your communication arrows, **become the customer** (as you did when viewing the furry dice) and see **your** offering through **their** eyes.

- Then and only then consider which communication methods are most likely to connect with them

Follow this formula and your chances of successfully connecting with your target audience will be considerably increased, as will your sales levels.

# CHAPTER 4

# CONNECTION, CONNECTION, CONNECTION!

*Converting consumers into customers…*
*YOUR customers!*

Time and again in this book you will notice I use phrases like, *'make a connection'*, or *'connect with'*, because that is really the bottom line for your business - succeed in making a connection between your offering and your *target audience* and you have at least a chance of making a sale.

Fail to do this however (as I did in my attempts to persuade you to buy my furry dice to help sell Rolls Royce cars) and you have **no** chance.

The next few chapters in this book are dedicated to helping you *connect* better and in doing so turning consumers, with free choice, into customers... **your** customers.

The three elements to consider are:

1.  Your offering

2.  Your target audience

3.  Successfully connecting the two

Before we move on to examine *your offering,* I want in this chapter to concentrate on *connection.* To do this I'm going to share with you two client case histories from **very** different markets and situations.

Although unalike in nearly all aspects, they are nevertheless identical in one; that of making a successful *connection* due to a strong understanding of the target audience and finding an appropriate way to make positive connection.

## 4.1 I didn't teach my Granny to suck eggs…
### …but I did teach her to use the Internet!

A number of years ago a good friend of mine who worked in IT, mainly developing websites, called me to say that the company he was employed by had just gone out of business.

He asked if I had any clients who may be looking for someone with his skills. I didn't, but went round to his home to see him anyway. After a bit of sympathy for his situation I then asked, "Why don't you go into business for yourself? You get on with people and obviously really know your way around a PC."

I think my suggestion took him a little by surprise and he responded, "Never thought about it. I don't really have much money to start a business and even if I did the big problem is getting customers."

I acknowledged this and asked him to give me a few days to think about my suggestion further. During that time I did some research into all things IT. As I mentioned at the beginning, this was several years ago, just when the real explosion of websites, email, webcams, social media and the like were beginning to take-off.

I knew my friend's skill mix, but what I needed was a niche for him in the market to apply it to and then find an inexpensive way to *connect* with potential target customers.

If I'm being honest, I wasn't getting very far until a headline caught my eye in a Sunday newspaper; it read, "Over 50's 'miss out' on Internet."

The basis of the story was that while younger members of our society were embracing the internet age and all it had to offer, many in the over 50 age group felt left behind and that they'd missed out on the opportunity.

Many understood the benefits of being better able to keep in touch with sons and daughters who had fled the nest to work in other parts of the UK and beyond, but felt that technology had moved on at such a pace that they didn't feel they could catch up.

I immediately called my friend and told him I thought I had the perfect business opportunity for him. Explaining the article I suggested that he offer his services to anyone who wanted the benefits that being connected on-line offer, but hadn't a clue where to start.

"You can take them right through the process, from the selection of the computer or laptop, its installation, loading of software, setting-up email accounts and even follow-on tuition on how to get the best out of it."

I went on to explain that although his service could in theory apply to any age group, that he should focus on the over 50's group. By doing this he would be tapping into a prime target audience and also help concentrate his communication efforts.

Although he liked the idea, his first question was, "How do we reach this target audience; advertising costs a fortune?"

The answer was by direct mail. My idea was to print 250 postcards; by having these digitally produced, this comparatively small print run still made economic sense. Then with the target audience in mind, drop them through letterboxes of estates occupied by more mature residents.

The final part in the jigsaw was what to say on the postcard? Here I decided to 'hire' a model to be photographed for the front of the card - his 76 year old **grandmother!**

I'd got this idea from the time I'd gone to his home and saw her on his PC. He had shown her the internet and she was having a fantastic time, a real *surfing granny!*

I've reproduced a visual on this page similar to the original card. The headline message was designed to make a *connection* with the *target audience*.

*'I didn't teach my granny to suck eggs, but I did teach her to use the Internet'.* This was followed on the back by, '...*and if I can teach her I can teach you!'*

I didn't teach my Granny to suck eggs, but I did teach her to use the internet!

The copy went on to explain that they had **not** missed the internet 'boat' and that he would guide them through the whole process.

Collecting the cards from the printer he immediately set off round the targeted estate, popping them through doors. He was on his third street when his mobile phone rang. It was from a house he had moments before delivered a postcard to.

A lady said her and her husband had only a couple of days before been speaking about the very subject of finding out how to 'get connected.' Within the hour he met them at a PC centre, helped them make their purchase and then installed it the same afternoon. While he was doing all this, the phone in his pocket rang twice more, again from recipients of the postcard.

Between those leads, tuition sessions, satisfied referrals and more leads from the postcards, his new business was able to get a foothold and grow.

*Connection made.*

## 4.2 Stopping infection...

*...a life-size example*

This example is not one from my small business casebook, but comes from work I did with a large hospital. Yet the principles of *connection* apply equally.

For any form of communication to work it must succeed in reaching the target audience on a number of levels. By this I mean **really grabbing** them in such a way that the key messages you want to get across will strike a chord with them.

More than this even, they must then feel sufficiently motivated to **act** - campaigns no matter how slick and clever will be for little if they fail to stir the target audience into action.

For this *connection* to happen, it is first essential to understand not just who the target audience is, but what they **think, feel,** and **want.**

The hospital in this story had a good record as far as infection control was concerned, but still felt that not enough visitors were heeding their request to wash their hands at the alcohol gel dispensers, before entering and again when leaving the hospital.

DISCLAIMER - this doctor
is NOT a doctor!

**Clean your hands**

Reducing and preventing the spread of infections is a really serious business and it wasn't that most people were deliberately ignoring this; there just wasn't enough impact to make the connection with them as they entered.

The solution we arrived at was quite literally a life size one! We photographed a senior nurse and produced a life size cut-out, requesting visitors to stop and wash their hands.

The impact of being confronted at the entrance by a senior nurse (albeit a cardboard one) making this request, made a dramatic difference and levels of gel being used soared. Other hospitals copied the idea using a variety of health professionals, including surgeons.

But why did it work? In my experience the overwhelming number of the general public really respect our nurses. We all appreciate and value the work they do for us and our families at the time of our need. We also care about those we visit and do not want to make their condition worse.

By understanding our **target audience** in this way, the idea of communicating with them by having a senior health professional ask for their help, succeeded in making the *connection* **and** motivating them to **act.** Visitors neither wanted to disrespect the nursing professional, nor disregard their request.

*Connection made.*

# CHAPTER 5

# MARKET SEGMENTATION OR THE BEST FETISH I EVER SAW!

*Positioning yourself in your marketplace*

This chapter is all about your chosen marketplace and more importantly where you sit within it.

When I first meet a start-up enterprise I ask them who the target audience for their product or service are. You'd be amazed at the number of times I get the response, "Well almost everyone." Well good luck with that! Where do you even **begin** to market to **everyone** and with what size of budget?!

It is so important to remember that no matter how much you wish it, you can't sell to everyone, no one can. The truth is that within every market there are companies offering different variations on the same theme, each designed to attract a different sector of that market.

Just think of the motor industry and the many different cars that are produced, each aimed at a specific type of customer.

What you have to do is work out which part of the market **your** offering fits best. This is the point I often make in lectures to start-up and small businesses. The problem is that as usual my profession have come up with a somewhat boring and academically threatening term for this, *'market segmentation'*.

In the past whenever I have shown a PowerPoint slide with that phrase on, the reaction of my audience was something like the photo on the top of the page opposite!

To zip things up a little I tried to show an orange split into segments to illustrate the concept in a more interesting way; did it work? Did it heck! Again the reaction was... Zzzzzz.

At this rate I was heading for a Nobel Prize in medicine - for curing insomnia.

Then one day I had an idea… a rather **bold** idea! I changed the slide to read, '*Market segmentation **OR** the best **fetish** I ever saw!*'

The shock in the room was matched only by the palpable change in mood…

I had finally succeeded in getting the attention of my audience... the only problem now was what to say next?!

I began by explaining that the Sex industry starts with a wide portal and then begins to subdivide into different parts of that market. Companies trading in the industry have to decide which part of the market their offering is best placed.

"Look, I'll show you!" I said, feeling like an overly keen professor delivering a practical biology class.

"Just supposing we enter 'sex' into the search engine, what do we get?" I rapidly followed this with, "**No** don't answer that! I'll tell you instead."

What I did get surprised me as much as I suspect it did them and maybe you too, it said: '*About 3,340,000,000 results*'. I can forgive them for the word 'about' at the beginning of that figure.

Now of course many of these will not be part of the 'sex' industry, so this time I entered a more probing phrase: '*sex website*'. The figure that came back again surprised me: 1,750,000,000. God what is going on out there and more to the point what am I *missing?!*

With my professional marketing hat on I returned to the point. How can anyone begin to cover such a size of marketplace; as it is bound (no pun intended) to be broken down into many more categories? It was the word 'categories' that then gave me the idea of next entering the search term '*sex fetish*' into the engine. The result: 202,000,000 - blimey!

Still at least we were now down in the hundreds of millions. Clearly however, if you are in the sex industry that is still too big a challenge to tackle, especially for a start-up company.

So finally I became even more precise in my search term by entering: 'unusual sex fetish'. This reduced the figure to 3,070,000.

Market segmentation is about breaking your marketplace down until you arrive at a point where you think your offering feels comfortable and manageable. Then you can look at what competition there is and how your product or service can better it.

My online 'research' (yes that's **all** it was!) took me one final step, as I decided to select at random one of the millions of unusual fetish websites to visit. I deliberately didn't look, just clicked the link.

The site I landed on took me completely by surprise and on the next page is the result!

DISCLAIMER: If you are under 18, of a nervous disposition, or easily shocked, please jump to the next section of this book. For everyone else (which is probably everyone!), turn the page and find out what I saw...

## ... ladies with their collars up!

Yes, the *'unusual fetish'* that I found via my searches was… wearing a shirt or coat with the collar turned up!

That's it, **brilliant!**

I just love the thought of a guy being invited back to the apartment of a lady he's been on a date with, only for her to say in seductive tones… "I'll just go and slip **out** of this shirt."

For him to then give the panicked response of, "**No!** Don't do that!" Then, trying to sound casual, he adds, "Just stay here and put your collar up."

Now as befits a marketing book this wonderful fetish actually brands itself! For instead of calling it *'a fetish for people who like seeing other people wearing collars up'*, they shorten this to, *'collar popping!'* Great name!

Now you'd imagine that if *collar popping* was your bag, you'd be satisfied with any photos of ladies wearing their collars up - but no!

* **Photograph:** My thanks go to Laura Jane Carson for modelling a man's shirt so well!

This fetish actually segments, even further.

You see the people who run sites for this fetish, **really** understand their subject **and** their target audience. So they have a dedicated section for those men who like *executive ladies* with collars up, one for those who like the *colour red* in collars and even one for those who adore the *country girl* look... gingham check shirts!

This is **really** good marketing; they don't try and roll all the options of their fetish up into one, but instead divide them into individual sections, so the target audience can immediately link to the one they most prefer.

This is similar to hotels that offer not only accommodation, but also conference facilities, wedding packages and so on. Each one of these has its own button on the website's home page so as to more easily connect the different target audiences.

By companies subdividing their offering in this way until they *connect* with a particular target audience, there is a better chance of visitors progressing from *consumer* to *customer*.

**Connection made.**

As a start-up business it is important therefore not to try and tackle an entire industry, but to segment or break your marketplace down until you find a niche you feel comfortable in, one that best suits your offering. In the case of the example in this chapter, it is **specialist knowledge** that leads them to understand what their target audience are looking for.

Before leaving our *collar popping* friends I do want to add one thing. The fetish community have a wonderful statement that encompasses the myriad of fetishes that exist, *'If you don't get it, you don't get it!'*

I think that statement, just like collar popping is great!

And, finally, finally, for lady readers, who feel this has all been a bit one-sided, I'm pleased to report that this particular fetish even has a following among women who enjoy seeing **men** with their collars up!

One male correspondent to a forum said that when he walks down a street with his collar up, he can tell from women's glances that they have and I quote, "A sparkle in their eyes and a tingle in their spines!"

Wow, look I mean if it's that easy... and please let's remember I am still single and getting on a bit - then let's give it a go...

'So ladies what do you think?

Any *sparkling* or *tingling* going on that I should know about?'

**No?**

Damn, I knew it was to good to be true! So much for market segmentation then!

## 5.1 Surviving the jungle!
### *Living alongside the BIG beasts*

From the last section we now know that whatever the overall marketplace heading; your offering must find its place within it. In a sense you will be in a marketplace within a marketplace.

If for example your business is making high quality, hand-made teddy bears for children, with personalised monogrammed sweaters; while being part of the massive Gifting industry, you will then potentially subdivide to the Toys sector and again to the Soft Toys market.

Even then you may not be finished because although you are technically in competition with every other soft toy producer, in reality the sector you are interested in is that of Teddy Bears and further still, those who can offer some form of personalisation. Because your product is hand-made and high quality, you will drill down further still, as you are only really aiming at the upper end of the market.

The danger is in not understanding your place and trying to take on market leaders from a bigger segment than just your own niche area. This bigger market can be truly like a *jungle*, with market leaders and those who are intent on challenging them.

Initially at least, this is **not** your role, so stay away from conflict that you can't win. There is an old proverb that says, "When elephants fight, the ants get hurt." I do not mean to be disparaging comparing start-up companies to ants, because as we will see in section 5.3, *size doesn't matter!*

Be proud of who you are, but **realistic** too.

## 5.2 A right caper...

*...or an ingredient for making money?*

I wasn't going to include this section in the book, but the person who it concerns insisted I should, which is really good of her.

The reason for my reticence is that this isn't a completed case history, but very much a *work in progress*, as it hasn't even launched. Nevertheless the completed work behind the scenes is so advanced that she feels confident enough to share the concept. I'm grateful, as it fits well into this chapter's debate of where you sit in your chosen marketplace.

We saw in the fetish section (5.0) how a market can drill down and down. Well if you think the search engine results for that were impressive try this one!

This lady, my nickname for her is *The Caperberry Queen*, has drilled down from her marketplace gateway of *'food'* which in the search engine I checked gave the following staggering figure: *About 3,550,000,000 results.*

Her place in the food marketplace is that of a single ingredient that can be found in many dishes and sauces. *The caper bush,* is a perennial winter-deciduous plant best known for the edible flower buds *(capers)*, often used as a seasoning, and also the fruit *(caper berry)*, both of which are usually consumed pickled.

Featuring bud and berry, her site will be a detailed resource on all things *caper*; from their history right the way through to the dishes each can be found in.

Additionally she has made a number of short videos and has compiled an *'A to Z'* of recipes, containing both the capers and the berries.

Her intention is to build visitor figures to her website by circulating articles to magazines and online food websites, asking only for a link to her site in return. As both her reputation and visitor numbers grow, so she will invite advertising from those food producers linked to the caper bud and berry.

This would make perfect sense from their viewpoint as the visitors to her site are also very much **their** target audience.

Once again like the fetish group, we have here an authoritative site focusing on a small segment of a much larger marketplace.

But as we will discuss in the next section this is **exactly** where small businesses can excel… at being **specialist.**

## 5.3 Size doesn't matter (honest!)...

### ...you're NOT 'small' - you're 'SPECIALIST'!

In this chapter we've seen examples of positioning within a subdivision of a much larger marketplace in order to gain a foothold.

Many start-up companies do this in order to attract a smaller, but more dedicated target audience. By having specialist knowledge and providing a committed service or product, they succeed in *making a connection.*

Many of the most successful companies I know have begun in this way and then once established, branched out into other associated areas.

I want to mention this now because I have seen time and time again new companies try to look bigger than they actually are and in my opinion it is often a mistake.

I remember once receiving an enquiry from an independent financial adviser - a one-man-financial-band. Yet when I saw his literature and read the wording it honestly made him look and sound like the *Bank of England.*

It turned out to be that while he was successful through his literature in winning appointments, when people scratched the surface they almost immediately realised he worked on his own and from home. Discovering this made them feel suspicious; not that there is anything wrong with working from home, or that **you** are the only person in your company, just please be upfront about it.

This man was one of the most knowledgeable on his subject I had ever come across and so I advised him to play on that strength by explaining he was a **dedicated specialist** in his field.

We changed his literature to match this message and although he initially found it harder to win appointments, when he did present, people knew exactly what they were getting and listened to his advice. It **worked** and his *closing ratio* showed a noticeable increase.

I think what happens in situations like this is that start-up and small businesses sometimes feel they lack credibility in the eyes of potential customers and so they try to '*big themselves up*' and act like they believe a large company would.

But here's the ironic bit; nearly every **big** business that has consulted me has wanted to act like a **small** one! The larger the company the more they want to reintroduce that one-to-one special relationship that so often exists only between small enterprises and their clients.

They know that people like to be treated as individuals and have their preferences remembered and catered for. That's why larger on-line retailers invest so much in their software that '*remembers and welcomes you back*' on each visit. They are trying to be **'small!'**

There is nothing to be ashamed about entering a market as a new player, quite the contrary. Your message is that you have seen what is on offer to consumers in your segment of a marketplace and after due consideration you believe your offering is better, or different; something fresh and exciting!

I would encourage you to consider using in your promotional literature, advertising or website phrases like, *'This is our business, our **only** business'*, indicating that you have gained considerable expertise in your field.

*Consult a specialist* is a stronger message than *deal with a bigger organisation,* which only offer a similar product/service to yours as an **add-on** and therefore may have less experience or expertise. This really comes into play when a customer requires advice, or if something goes wrong.

In other words because you are devoting your **entire** working life to a specific business you have earned the right to be regarded as an expert in that field.

Another winning line, if it applies to your type of business is that of, *'A family-run business'*. People trust family businesses, seeing them as committed and honest because they are entrenched in the community they serve.

There are other significant advantages too over bigger companies, which being small in size can give. For a start you can move **faster,** no red tape and layers of management to go through to get a decision. If you see a trend developing, especially local, you can move much quicker than the larger juggernaut companies to fulfil it.

As the king of your own small empire, you may decide to open longer hours than they do, or offer an add-on service that again is not always easy for them to quickly react to.

I'd like to end this section by giving an example from a client of mine that I first met over a decade ago.

I was consulted by a small independent estate agent in Cramlington, north east of England, whose principal had been selling houses there since 1977. Nevertheless as housing in the area had developed rapidly, not one, but three national firms of estate agents had also opened in close proximity.

Although very confident in his service, he asked whether there was anything additional they should perhaps do in the way of marketing themselves.

Before deciding on any course of action, I asked if I could play the role of a prospective house buyer and ask him some questions about the properties they were representing and likely trend in their valuations, given the areas in which they were situated.

Over the next half an hour he gave me the history behind where each house was sited, whether there had ever been any serious flooding, what were the crime rates, what schools and youth facilities existed and what was the area's overall reputation.

He answered in full all my questions in a most impressive way, not deliberately trying to sell to me as such, but just pleased to share his extensive knowledge for my benefit, as he would any prospective client.

What's more he had also shared this knowledge with his staff, so each was able to offer the very best in terms of advice.

I then went to visit each of the three national chains and asked similar questions. What I was greeted by were a number of mainly younger members of staff, who were polite but only really able to hand me an information sheet on each property and answer general questions about the area; but crucially none of the **really** in-depth issues.

People often say that you don't really know an area until you live there, but getting as much detailed intelligence on it is the next best thing. Sadly from each of the three national estate agents this was to a large extent missing.

When I returned to my client I told him that in my opinion he should simply introduce, at minimal cost, a short sentence on all advertising, stationery, literature, window displays, property detail cards and even the way they introduced themselves to every new enquiry.

The short statement went as follows, '**No** one knows Cramlington, like **we** know Cramlington'.

By promoting at every opportunity this unique strength of **specialist** local knowledge, they had their own precious niche in the market and one that no matter how big their competitors were, none could match.

Following a recent conversation with the owner, I'm pleased to report that his business is still thriving and that, '**No one** knows Cramlington like **we** know Cramlington', is still very much their mantra.

So the message from this section is: please celebrate your arrival on the scene and for small read **specialist!**

**Photograph:** My thanks goes to Matt Kay for turning up early one Saturday morning to have his photograph taken with a man he'd never met before who was standing on a box! Thanks Matt, well beyond the call of duty!

## 5.4 Positioning this book...
   *...where to Stand-up?*

Finally in this chapter, you are not the only new kid on the block; *I am too!*

As a new enterprise we've spoken about the importance of positioning within a subdivision of a much larger marketplace in order to gain a foothold.

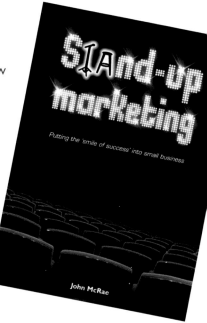

We've confirmed that while this may attract a smaller audience in terms of numbers, that is more than compensated for because those you will attract are the **right** target audience for your offering. By having **specialist** knowledge and providing a **dedicated** service or product for this target group, there is a greater likelihood of *making a connection.*

Well even a marketing man with a new book has to have a place within a market. I have gone through the same exercise as I'm recommending you do. My portal was *Business books*, this quickly subdivided to *Marketing books*.

Now at this point it may appear tempting for me to pitch my book to **anyone** in business, regardless the size of their enterprise. This would give me a larger number of potential people and companies to target.

However while some concepts and examples in this book may trigger ideas for established medium to large enterprises, they should already be clear on the fundamental building blocks of marketing.

So instead I am devoting this book to *start-up* and *small* enterprises. I am targeting this segment of the marketplace because I believe I have something to offer, something **different**, maybe in some ways even **better** than what currently exists.

If you were attracted to this book because the terms *start-up* and *small business* were mentioned in connection with it, then my marketing has succeeded in helping this book reaching its intended destination; **you!**

*Connection made.*

# CHAPTER 6

# TWO VERY DIFFERENT WAYS TO DEPART THIS WORLD!

*'Brand' and 'branding' – what's the difference and why the big deal?*

The word **brand** has been around for a very long time, being derived from the Old Norse word *brandr,* 'to burn'. We know it best from cattle, when one owner would brand his herd with a distinguishing mark for purposes of identification.

In today's commercial world, the word *brand* is well known by businesses and consumers alike, but what exactly does it mean for **you** and your enterprise and what is the difference between *brand* and *branding* - and why the heck does it matter so much?

The first question to nail right away is, "I'm only a small start-up business; so does this chapter apply to me?" My answer is simply, **yes**. Not only should your enterprise have a *brand* it **must** have one. Even a one-man-band micro business has to not only have a *brand,* but a *distinctive* one too.

Just like cattle that were branded for purposes of differentiation from other herds, your business also must be clearly defined for what it represents; it must **stand out.** Failure to achieve this will mean a struggle for survival.

If you go online and search for the definition of both *brand* and *branding,* you will find some interesting variations on a theme, some quite involved.

In the following sections I will give you my own take on what each word means to me, in relation to **your company.** I hope to do this in a straightforward way that you will not only be able to relate to, but I hope begin to also apply to your enterprise.

In the previous chapter we looked at your place in the market. The purpose of **this** one is to now begin to look at what makes your offering not just specialised, but **special** in fact I'll go further, **unique.**

So before you begin to spend money communicating your product or service to potential customers, it is important to know **what** you are going to say that best describes your offering and critically **how** that will make a *connection* with your target audience.

*A connection that will lead to* **more sales!**

## 6.1 What is a 'brand?'
### *It's what's on the* **inside**

When reading this section please begin the process of considering what the *brand* of your own company might be.

To explain the difference between a *brand* and *branding,* I'd ask you to imagine your company as a human body. Your **brand** is what is **inside** you; it is your heart, your soul, your beliefs and values, your personality, your passion.

### It is what drives you.

The French have a wonderful expression which sums this up very well indeed, *'raison d'être'* meaning, **reason for existence.**

These attributes are what make you as a person who you are; they are what help make you unique. The same has to be true of your company; it must resonate with **your** values and begin to show its own character. Because from the values of your brand come **reputation.**

Imagine consumers seeing your literature or website for the first time; what kind of world are they going to see? What messages will you give them?

Think of your *brand* as the **DNA** of your company, it's what makes it **unique.** It defines and explains what it represents.

So what **will** it stand for? What **is** your world, your *brand?*

You have chosen to go into business, a massive step; in doing so you will be committing not only your finances, but also your time, energy, skills, knowledge and ethos. All of these must contribute towards you developing a winning and sustainable *brand,* one that will gain a deserved favourable reputation among consumers, which will help greatly to convert them into customers.

***Your brand is your company's heartbeat; even more... its spirit.***


## 6.2 Vive la difference...
### ...the *real* brand of France?

A *brand* doesn't only have to apply to a product or service. Critically, as discussed in the last section it begins with the **company** that produces it.

But even outside of companies, *brands* exist in different fields. A *brand,* like a defining characteristic, can relate to areas as diverse as political doctrines, sports teams, music genres, cities and even countries.

In fact I would like to share with you what I consider to be the *real* brand of one country in which I've spent much of my working life - France!

On arrival at *Charles de Gaulle* airport in Paris, for years I have been bombarded by images that French tourism would have me believe is the real *brand* or personality of their country.

Iconic landmarks such as: the *Eiffel Tower*, historic palaces like *Versailles*, beautiful chateaux, remarkable art, and of course gastronomic delights, including some amazing patisseries. Now while these clearly all exist, I've always felt that the **real** *brand* of France was somehow **more.**

For the real *brand* of a country, spend time with the **people** who live there. Of course France is a big country and people's attitudes can vary from region to region. I have spent much time in the *Loire Valley* where the hospitality and warmth of the welcome is the best I've ever experienced.

Although this for me is **more** the *brand* of France, it only **really** came into sharp focus when I read on a news internet website the following headline:

### '*French riot police outraged over plans to ban beer and wine with their meals*'

I smiled when I saw this because a friend of mine who lived in Paris for two years had once told me that the best show in town was the riot police in action with water cannons **after** lunch!

The news story went on to say, that for riot police, the long-cherished tradition of drinking alcohol with their lunch was about to end.

The story made headline news and a government minister was wheeled out to face the media, explaining in firm tones that in France there was already a no-alcohol rule, *"In French law, alcohol is banned while employees are at work…"*

Well that's clear enough, until he added, "…well, except for wine, beer, apple cider, pear cider…"

Now **THAT,** for me at least, is the **real** brand of *France!*

A country that believes 'a *small drink*' can enhance social and even business relations - and you know what? *I believe it* **does!**

I have done business in France for many years and in that time much corporate bonding has been improved over a glass of Bordeaux. So as far as I am concerned, long may their *brand* of conviviality and bon-accord prevail.

**Vive la France! Vive la difference!**

## 6.3 What is 'branding?'
### It's what's on the **outside**

In section 6.1 we compared your company to a human body, explaining that its **brand** is what is on the inside.

Now comparing your business to the same human body, we turn to what is visible on the **outside;** for example clothing, hair, make-up, jewellery, accessories.

**Stylisation.**

A person's styling often gives a strong indication of their inner personality and companies are no different.

Let's remember that before a consumer who comes across your offering actually finds out about your inner self, your *brand*, they will first of all see what is on the outside. It is therefore critical that there is a synergy between the two, *brand* and *branding*.

This is important because with so little time nowadays, people often make snap judgements on what they first see. If it doesn't **look** like what they are seeking they will move on and you will have lost a potential customer.

Remember the example of Rolls Royce and the pink furry dice in section 3.1. In that instance the two didn't *fit*, they jarred and were simply way out of sync. If people didn't know what Rolls Royce stood for and had come across the pink furry dice first, there is no way they would have associated it with such a prestigious product.

Your branding or corporate identity is therefore very much the outer face of the inner brand, its *representative*. As such, careful thought has to be given to what image it portrays in the eyes of the consumer.

We will discuss *market research* later in the book and this is one area where it often pays to take target audience soundings. From your outer *branding* what inner *brand* messages are consumers picturing?

Everything from font, colours and images that are used to portray your company have to be considered to make sure they **work in partnership with your brand.**

## 6.4  Way to go!
### *An appropriate exit?*

I'd like to present in this section an imaginary example of a *brand* and *branding* illustrating why unless in sync with each other they simply won't work.

As mentioned in 6.3 when considering your corporate identity it is vital that you ensure it is **appropriate**, for the *brand* of your company.

Let's say that you decided to open a new business offering *funeral services*. As we know you must first consider what your *brand* for this service will be.

If your business is to be called **Bereavement Funeral Services** and

**specialises** in offering a very **traditional** type of funeral, then it could well include: a service with scripture readings, prayers, and organ music, possibly a procession to the cemetery, with your staff attired in traditional black dress code.

Taken together your *brand* would be a service offering a very dignified and solemn exit from this world.

If this were the case then it would probably be best **not** to have the following for your *branding*...

A font that is called *Jokerman*, a screaming day-glow orange colour and a hand enthusiastically waving **'bye'** as the departed makes their final exit!

Just like the pink furry dice of earlier in this book that imagery jars totally with the *brand;* it doesn't fit, it isn't appropriate and gives out wildly confusing messages.

However let's now assume that your new funeral services company decides instead, that its *brand* will tap into the mood among many of today's younger generations who **don't want** a traditional funeral, full of solemnity and sadness, with people crying at their demise.

Instead they'd rather make people **smile** and have those attending wear bright clothes, play music that they loved and make the whole service a **celebration** of their life.

If your company facilitated this type of departure from the world, then its identity could reflect this *brand,* perhaps being named, 'Smile as you go'.

Its *branding* could then look like **this**...

Now it is entirely **fitting** to have a screaming orange colour and a font called *Jokerman*. Suddenly both work, they are suitable. Even the hand waving *'bye'* works because it is designed to convey that the *brand* of your service is light, bright and happy.

So now we can see that you can have two companies competing in the **same sector,** offering the **same service** (despatching people) in the **same geographic location**, even at the **same price** - yet **totally different** in their *approach*, dependent on their *brand*.

Clearly each of these approaches is aimed at different audiences and here you need to be certain that your *brand* will be able to attract a sufficiently large target group to make your business successful.

In the next chapter of the book we'll look at other examples from small companies who faced the dilemma of what their **brand** was, what made them different, what made them better?

It's time for **you** to decide which way to go...

## 6.5 Together in harmony...
### ...brand and branding

In the last section of this chapter I'd like to present examples of *branding* that I have produced **following** careful consideration of what the company or organisation's *brand* is. They are in sync and so have a powerful effect.

As your business grows you will see that by closely linking your *brand* and *branding*, you will have a great asset, the bedrock of your company.

I've included some notes about how the final *branding* solution was arrived at and my sincere thanks go to the companies and organisations who have generously allowed their example to be included here because they want to help others succeed - fantastic!

**Fast Forward Now**

fastforwardnow.com
*education to enterprise*

Headed up by Angela McLean, award-winning entrepreneur and enterprise education consultant, Fast Forward Now has worked with individuals and small business start-ups locally, nationally and internationally, developing their enterprise skills and supporting their growth.

At a time when universities and local authorities are becoming increasingly focused on delivering enterprise and entrepreneurship education to graduates and postgraduates, Fast Forward Now provides a bridge from academic teaching and research provided by the institutions, to one that incorporates practical business experience.

When I worked on the branding with Angela I had a strong feeling that her company's brand involved taking students with absolutely no entrepreneurial experience to a state of becoming 'enterprise-ready'. Many of her students have gone on to benefit from her approach and open successful businesses.

I chose 'stars' to include in her branding as representative of the aspirations of her students, each of whom is 'reaching for the stars' in terms of starting their own business. As with many projects, the website tag (in this case .com) was incorporated, so the branding is also the website address.

### Health and Wellbeing

 Health and Wellbeing

One of the organisations I have been most proud to be associated with over the years is not in fact a small business, but one of the most progressive and successful NHS Trusts in the UK.

Northumbria Healthcare NHS Foundation Trust manage hospital, community health and adult social care services in Northumberland and hospital and community health services in North Tyneside. It is recognised as being one of the country's top trusts, leading the way in many healthcare initiatives.

The project shown here was one aimed at benefitting the health and wellbeing of their workforce. Human Resources and Occupational Health teams worked on producing a range of support services that staff could tap in to.

However, the organisation was keen to ensure that staff could do this when **they** wanted to and were not being pressurised into using the services, or being preached at.

Instead the approach was to empower staff, so when **they** decided the time was right; the Trust would support them in a number of ways to achieve their goal.

For example their support service for those wishing to stop smoking was labelled: '*Time to quit?*' Note the use of the question mark, instead of an exclamation mark. By including this it became a question, not any kind of command; saying instead when **you** decide the time is right to quit, we are here to offer support.

That then was the project's brand - supporting staff in the choices they made and at a time that suited them. A campaign of '*When you are ready*' reinforced this message.

When it came to matching the branding to the brand we chose a version of the power-on icon as used on PCs, televisions and other electrical devices. I felt this symbol was appropriate as before accessing any of the services these devices have to offer, the user first has to push the button - when **they** want; the identical principle behind the *Health and Wellbeing* scheme.

## Tenerife.co

# Tenerife.co

Tenerife is known as the *'Island of eternal spring'* and this sunshine element is a major part of both *brand* and *branding* in this example.

By adding the domain tag at the end (.co) it combines as the website address. You will see more than one example of this type of combining name and site address in the book and I'd encourage you to consider it for your own branding. Of course in this case I was able to use the 'o' of the .co to good effect, as the sun! The colours chosen to reflect the Mediterranean.

## Move it Fast

# MOVE IT FAST ))

A number of years ago I worked on a branding for a company that offered a service to rival that of estate agents.

By cutting a lot of the red tape normally associated with selling properties, this company was able to potentially reduce significantly the time a property remained on the market.

They asked me to give the service a name and branding. At the time no one in the property market was using the name 'Move it fast' and by adding the 'fast forward' chevrons at the front, the image became one of acceleration.

In fact the font we used was called 'Accelerator' and indeed gives the impression of speed. As the majority of customers for this service were likely to be under 30, we used a modern orange for the colour.

## Garbeau

Jessica McLean has breathed life into what used to be the rather traditional and 'clubby' world of made-to-measure shirts.

In the past having one of these garments tailored could mean a very significant cost and a shirt that was frankly a little old fashioned in terms of style.

Now Jessica offers a range of stylish casual, business and dress wear shirts **and** with a twist! Not only can you design your own made-to-measure shirt from a wide range of quality fabrics and shirt design options, but you can personalise it by adding your initials on the cuff or pocket.

You can even add a personal message inside the collar which is a lovely touch, for example on a wedding day shirt.

With such a tailored service, in every respect, I worked with Jessica to develop a branding to match. The name *Garbeau* is an amalgam of the words 'garb', meaning a distinctive style or form of clothing and 'beau', a man who is concerned with his dress and appearance.

We twinned this with a signature font, called Garabata, to emphasise personalisation. The distinctive colour combination was chosen by Jessica - well after all she is a fashion designer!

**Hidden Markings**

## HIDDEN MARKINGS

As a friend of mine has told me for years, in security, *'what is visible is either copyable or destructible.'*

This is something that one of my clients takes very seriously. In fact they stand or fall by it.

Their business is the production of invisible markings that identify genuine products and also offer traceability to source information.

So seriously do they take *hidden security* that they go to great lengths to protect their own company's identity, which has been changed for this book.

Their branding consists of an ellipse containing the letters HM. For this book I have shown this with a drop shadow effect, but in reality both ellipse and letters are embossed onto their business stationery.

In effect saying *we are here*, but only visible under certain conditions; a strong connection between their *brand* and *branding.*

## Berwick Garden Centre

When asked to produce branding for England's most northerly garden centre, the solution I arrived at with the owner Nick Crabbie was one that will have any gardeners reading this scratching their heads. The reason is, the plant we used for the logo doesn't exist - I made it up!

However there is a good reason behind that decision. The garden centre, situated on the outskirts of Berwick upon Tweed majors on both indoor and outdoor plants and so we decided to produce a hybrid of the two. The base of the logo is a terracotta colour to represent the earth.

## The Kingfisher's Rest

At the same time as producing the branding for Berwick Garden Centre I was asked to do likewise for a magnificent new restaurant that was opening within it.

While Nick and I were walking round the centre he drew my attention to a beautiful Kingfisher. "You'll see them around here, along the River Tweed." It was as if it was a sign and we decided there and then that *The Kingfisher's Rest* was the perfect name.

It is a name and branding that is much admired by those who use the restaurant.

**Fresh and Filling**

A longstanding client and one of the best entrepreneurs I've ever met recently called me to say he had an idea for a new concept of take-away eatery. He explained that while people like the concept of healthy, fresh food, that many feel this often equates to also *'going hungry'*.

He went on to say that he intended to produce satisfying meals with quality fresh ingredients, "A sort of *fresh and filling* approach," he added. "So I need you to come up with a name for me please."

I replied that he had already done that! Four weeks later *'Fresh and Filling'* was launched. The identity produced was simple and told the story of his offering, the word fresh in a vegetable green and the word filling in a bold font. Again we added the .com so the branding also advertised the website address.

## Celebrate summer!

One of the more unusual requests I've had in the last year was *branding* for posters, leaflets and banners for a community summer event in **Canada** (thanks to the Internet we truly operate in a global market!).

The event was the first of its type in the community and the organisers were keen that its *brand* should be a mix of *summer fun* for kids, linked to messages of *fitness* and *safety*. Therefore a fun fair was supplemented by such activities as bike safety workshops, sports demonstrations and presentations by the *Ottawa Fire Department.*

As we received the request with a very short deadline, we opted for a bright colourful branding; using a font called Billy which associates with kids, a summer blue backdrop and red and yellow sun colours for the *Celebrate Summer* header.

To stay with the **safety** theme we used a stock graphic of a sun holding a tube of sun protection cream, as a subliminal reminder to both parents and children to *cover up* in the fierce summer sun.

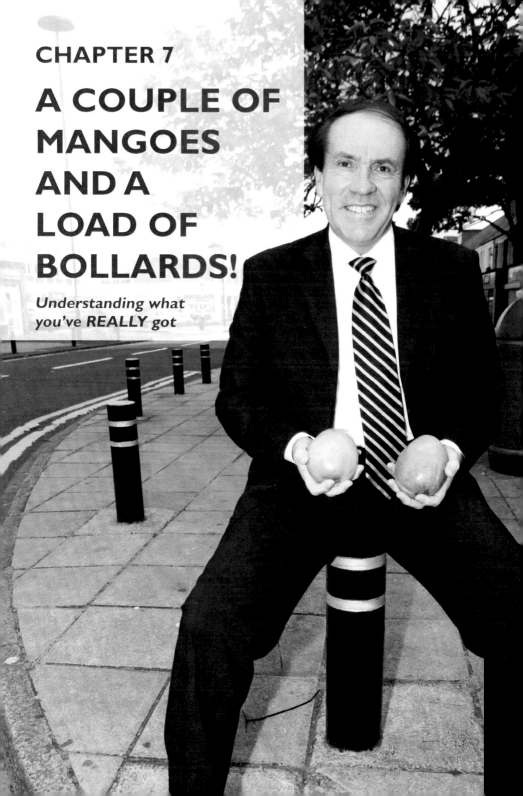

# CHAPTER 7

# A COUPLE OF MANGOES AND A LOAD OF BOLLARDS!

*Understanding what you've REALLY got*

I hope the headline for this chapter caught your eye, as this is one of the most important in the book. I did consider, for reasons you will shortly see, swapping the chapter heading for a shorter one of just two words, *'Why you?'*

We will come to the *'couple of mangoes'* in the next section, but first let's talk… *a load of bollards!*

In the last chapter we saw how important your *brand* is in defining your company's ethos and *uniqueness*. Start-up and small companies often have difficulty in explaining their uniqueness to prospective customers and yet doing so is the cornerstone of success.

When I am invited to go and see a company, I begin by finding out a little of their background, length of time in business, nature of their offering and so on.

After a few minutes, I then ask a very short, direct question, that often takes them by surprise, **"Why you?"**

I then repeat the question, but in a slightly different way, "Why should I buy from **you** as opposed to one of your competitors? After all as a new company you have a short track record compared to longer standing competitors' - so **why you,** what is it that you have that they don't?"

This for me is the absolute killer question in business. Fail to answer this and you will struggle.

That may sound dramatic, but if you think about it why should **you** spend **your** money with a new supplier that you don't know and one that can't give you a reason why their offering is **better** than what currently exists?

In response to my question a small business owner will often begin to describe what their business **does.** That is all very well, but I often know what a plumber, or accountant, or driving instructor, or sandwich shop or a myriad of other small businesses **do.**

What I want to know is, as a *consumer* with free choice, why I should choose **you!**

If you have not yet started in business, make this question your starting point. If you are already in business use it to test how you explain your offering to the market; how do **you** answer the question, *"Why You?"*

Now we get to the **bollards** bit!

A number of years ago I was invited to go and see an engineering company in the Midlands who had a problem; I didn't know the exact nature of which until I got there. Actually this wasn't a start-up company but a 20 year old traditional engineering one with a workforce of about 15.

However they had ventured into a **new** product category and this was why I had been summoned.

Over one of the strongest coffees I've ever been given - more robust even than their steel - the business owner explained his problem. The engineering market is a very competitive sector, with profit margins being continually squeezed.

Then one day out of the blue he had received a call from his local council asking if he could produce some *bollards* in a hurry. Apparently a nearby shopping centre had been hit by ram-raiders over the weekend who had smashed into an electrical shop window, loaded their van with goods and driven off. So now the council wanted to install bollards to prevent similar incidents in the future.

They wanted them mounted in as fast a turnaround time as possible to placate the concerns of their tenants, the centre's store owners.

Although never having made an actual bollard before the owner not wishing to turn away business affirmed he could make them and **then** got all his workers round to decide how this could best be done! The **real** spirit of enterprise!

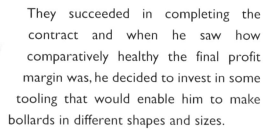

They succeeded in completing the contract and when he saw how comparatively healthy the final profit margin was, he decided to invest in some tooling that would enable him to make bollards in different shapes and sizes.

Although he was able to defray the cost somewhat by producing part of the tooling himself, it was still a very sizeable outlay and one that required a fairly quick return on investment.

To help generate business for this new line he had one of his workforce obtain brochures from other bollard manufacturers. He then produced his own; similar to those he had received and mailed them out to the tendering and contracts departments of councils across the country.

When I went to see him it was some 2 months after this and he explained to me that to date, apart from his local council, he had not been successful in winning an order, nor even gaining approval to go on any tender lists.

I asked about his competitors and he produced their brochures, laying them out on the desk. I browsed through them and said that, they all looked pretty much the same as his. He replied, *"Well I suppose they are pretty much the same as ours."*

He explained some bollards are more decorative, others heavier, similar to what he had produced to stop the ram-raiders, but most manufacturers can produce either.

So then I asked him the killer question. Holding up the brochures of the other bollard manufacturers in one hand and then his in the other, "Why you? Why should a council buy your bollards as opposed to one of your competitors; especially as you have less of a track record than them?"

He couldn't give a definitive answer, instead saying that he would provide *quality* and a *good service*. I told him that most customers would take that as a minimum requirement and that all his competitors promise the same anyway.

I continued by asking if his bollards were at the most expensive, or lower end of the market. He replied that they **could** be made to a higher or lower specification if requested; again, similar to most of his competitors.

I next suggested that perhaps his bollards had some kind of unique, super-duper anti-corrosion make-up, to stop them rusting if dogs pee on them? Again he replied well he could probably achieve this, but admitted that so could his competitors.

We tried other angles but with the same outcome. Whatever he could do, so could his competitors.

So again I repeated my initial question, "Why then should I buy your bollards as opposed to anyone else's?"

He finally had to admit that there **wasn't** a unique reason he could think of as to why his bollards were better than others, who were more established in the market place; and **that** was his problem.

He had not considered his *brand* and the advantage it gave the target audience before investing heavily in this new division of his business.

Selling is about giving people enough reasons to say *'yes'* and this he had failed to do. It is after all, hardly the greatest of battle cries, *'Buy from us; we're the **same** as everyone else!'*

I spent the next hour looking more closely at his offering, questioning each aspect, searching for something *special* or *unique*. It was only when I asked him about how long it would take to fulfil an order, from the point of receiving it that the mood changed.

This time he didn't hesitate, "Even if we were busy, the benefit of having the tooling is that once set up we can pop them out pretty quickly, and in fact I would feel very safe guaranteeing them in 3 working days."

I was a little taken aback by this and said, he hesitated and admitted he wasn't sure and so asked the young guy who had got the brochures from the other bollard producers. His reply stunned both me and the owner of the company.

"About 3 **weeks.**"

And **he** had just told me that he could supply them in 3 **days.**

Now bearing in mind the one order he had received, was requested as a matter of **urgency,** it immediately struck both him and I that there would again be circumstances when councils and other organisations would want them in a hurry. Suddenly the penny dropped, he had his '**why me**', his **brand**, his **unique** selling proposition.

It was at that point I witnessed the very best bit of selling I have ever seen in my life - mainly because it wasn't really selling, just sheer **conviction.**

He got the list of councils they had written to. Then picking up the phone, he dialled the first name on the list, got through to the appropriate person in tendering and said: "I simply have to introduce myself to you, as we have got something that could be of real benefit to you and it is important I make you aware of it."

He went on to explain that although he had written to them recently, he had omitted to mention one key fact - that they can supply bollards in just 3 days, whereas the industry norm is about 3 weeks.

Based on this new information, he asked if his company could now go on the tender list, as he felt that this unique benefit may at some point be very useful to them.

The man at the other end of the phone said, provided this was put in writing to him, the answer was **'yes!'**

### So what had changed?

The owner of the engineering company had invited me to his company, thinking I would perhaps produce a new brochure, or consider a better corporate identity, or view his website offering. Instead the only thing that really happened was that the owner suddenly understood **'why him'**. In an instant he had become aware of what he **really** had, a clear advantage over everyone else in the industry.

What was special about his *brand* was **speed,** which others couldn't match. Realising this he was motivated to feel that he, **'simply had to introduce himself'** to his target audience because he knew what he had may be of **real benefit** to them. He felt he had a sense of duty to tell them.

This is the feeling I am asking you to have with your offering; that feeling of *simply having to introduce yourself* to those you know can benefit. It is a wonderful feeling when you know you have something; an edge that others don't.

I often see *'How to sell'* courses advertised, to help close more deals. Well for me just having that passionate feeling of wanting to introduce yourself will carry you a long way toward success. No longer are you *campaigning,* you are **crusading.**

Remember too, it is when you don't have that feeling of having something unique that **price** becomes a more important issue and pressure increases to reduce prices.

The feeling of simply *having to introduce yourself* to your target audience is the test I would therefore ask you to consider for **your** brand.

Do **you** feel like kicking down doors to tell the good news of how you can help your target audience? If the answer to that is **'no'**, then can I please ask you to review your offering in terms of benefit to your target audience, because if **you** don't feel that way how the heck can you expect **them** to?

## 7.1 Pulp fiction?
### A **real** story of marketing mangoes

I have to repeat my gratitude to those companies who have allowed part of their story to be told in this book, as it may help other companies just starting out. Most of these stories however are ones of success; and it's always easier to tell a tale of triumph.

This chapter however is a little different in that it is a 'work in progress' story and so I cannot say that it will ultimately end in success. As such I have not named the product, or the company. *The owners nevertheless are happy for some of the details* to be relayed to you in the hope that it may help focus your thinking regarding your own product or service. How wonderful an attitude is that?

The importance of this story, just like the 'bollards' example in the last chapter, is understanding exactly what it is that your product or service has, in terms of benefitting your **target audience**. In particular what advantages can you offer that improves on the options currently available in your market place.

Although the company in question described themselves on their business card and literature as an *'agro trading company'* and a *'new UK start-up enterprise'*, I later discovered that the story actually begins way before that in an orchard in Devgad, western Ghats of Maharashtra, India.

The soil in this part of the country is rich in minerals that support the growth of the tree cells and together with nourishing environmental conditions, is perfect for growing a type of mango called *Alphonso*. This mango is regarded as 'the king', looking more attractive in comparison to other varieties due to its yellow colour, orange tinge and reddish hue at the base of its stem.

The positive consequence of all these supportive factors is the rich colour, flavour, taste and thick pulp that this mango delivers. It is that word 'pulp'

that now drives much of this story, for the company's business was the importation of *Alphonso* mangoes in pulp form rather than the whole fruit, or in tins. The pulp being sealed in aluminium pouches.

Although the company considered selling either directly to the public or through a vast network of independent food outlets in the UK, their infrastructure would not easily support this type of business model.

Instead their optimum route for gaining entry to the UK market is via the major supermarkets, albeit with a greater squeeze on their margins.

When I first met the company they had just completed a first round of presentations to two large UK supermarket chains - and these had not gone well, with little reported interest being shown. This was serious news, as this small group of supermarket buyers act as the gateway between the company and millions of potential UK consumers. Failure to convince them and the gate would remain firmly closed.

I began our discussions by establishing where they saw their product in terms of positioning in the marketplace. They felt that it was a premium product that would sit best mid to top end of the market, with target consumers being in the 25-60 age range, with around 80% being women.

This definition appeared to be supported by market research, albeit on a limited scale, that they had undertaken.

I wanted to get to the heart of why the two supermarket buyers had rejected the product, without even seriously entering into any pricing negotiations. The company felt the lack of interest seemed to split evenly into two areas:

1. The buyers didn't seem to grasp the benefits of the product.

2. They seemed to lack confidence that they would be dealing with a *start-up agro trading company.*

I then asked the company to explain the benefits of their product. There were four headline points in their presentation which were:

- 100% natural mango

- Part of your 5-a-day

- No e-numbers

- No citric acid

Looking at these I began to see the problem. Putting myself in the position of their target audience i.e. a supermarket buyer there was nothing in that list that really leapt out and grabbed me as being different, nothing that really excited me and nothing that gave me comfort that dealing with this *start-up agro trading company* would be a good bet.

And that is a shame, because as I am about to demonstrate this is a **fantastic** product that deserves a place on the UK's supermarket shelves.

In selling you have to give potential buyers enough reasons to say 'yes'. To do that successfully you have to begin by putting yourself in their position and see your offering through *their* eyes. You also have to know what options the potential buyer currently has open to them and then give the clear reasons why your offering provides something better.

Achieve that and you will have gone a long way to making a sale. Fail and your chances are minimal.

So I began by *'thinking as a supermarket buyer'*, and in doing so before I even consider getting to the negotiations nitty-gritty, I first need **comfort** that the company I am about to consider introducing to my chain will not let it down - or more to the point let **me** as the buyer down, thereby having an adverse effect on my career prospects!

Clearly being a start-up company with no track record is not great for comfort and an *agro trading company* sort of sounds like a 'middle-man' operation, again difficult because the supermarket will not be dealing with the source.

With those thoughts in my mind I turned to my client and began by asking them where exactly the mango pulp comes from. Their answer nearly dropped me from my chair!

"Our orchard," was the unexpected response. Now I kind of figured that the mangoes came from an orchard, but it was the introduction of the word **'our'** that changed everything.

"**Our** orchard," I asked, "you mean **you** are the source supplier of the mangoes?"

Then the story, the **real** story began to unfurl. It transpired that not only does the orchard belong to their family, but it has done for nigh on 100 years!

**Now** we have a completely different picture! Instead of being a *start-up agro trader,* which frankly made them sound a bit like a *Del Boy* character who *'could do you a few mangoes mate,'* they were actually mango farmers of 100 years standing, 100 years' experience of soil and crop management, with impeccable traceability to source credentials.

More than this they have practiced a co-operative farming philosophy, with full corporate responsibility toward sustainability, long before such concepts were labelled.

As for the start-up company bit, well this was done to better manage and support the UK stockists as a commitment from them to ensure that the supermarket buyers had a point of contact in this country.

Now with the credibility of the company better understood, what about the product? We repeated the exercise, this time focusing on their offering and how it compared with what currently exists. This is what I found.

### 100% natural mango pulp

I began by clarifying that by 100% natural their pulp contained no preservatives and they confirmed this to be the case. I then asked, perhaps a little too bluntly, "So what? Surely other mango products including tinned pulp are the same; otherwise you would be shouting from the rooftops that you are offering a 'first' on the market?"

A long silence followed, during which I realised that I had hit 'the mango on the head with a dessert spoon'. It was indeed a **first,** a unique selling point they had not considered mentioning - simply because they were too close to the situation and had not stepped back and viewed their offering through the eyes of someone who knew nothing about it.

Now it became even more exciting because what they were offering supermarket buyers was a genuine first and buyers *love* 'firsts'. Their message to those buyers was a simple one, 'give your supermarket's customers the first opportunity in the UK to enjoy the health benefit of 100% natural mango pulp.'

## Taste

But of course the absence of preservatives is not only a health benefit, it is also a **flavour** one! When the mangoes are taken from the orchard to be skinned, pulped and sealed in the aluminium pouches, the entire process takes under half a day. Therefore when a customer in the UK opens the pouch in their home, they are savouring the smell and taste of **fresh,** natural *Alphonso* mango, just hours old - fabulous!

## Availability

Now we come to comparisons with actual *Alphonso* mangoes which are available in UK supermarkets. However they are **only** available for a short window of just two months in the year, whereas my client's mango pulp is available to shoppers year-round.

## Shelf life

The next benefit really took me by surprise and was yet another that had not been mentioned in the initial presentation to buyers.

Due to the process of vacuum sealing, the shelf life of the product is an amazing 18 months - this without the need for refrigeration!

Of course this is a real winning benefit for both supermarket buyer and shopper. For the buyer it means they have one and a half years to move the product and so the risk of stocking it lessens very considerably, especially when one considers that the natural fruit goes off after two weeks. Likewise this benefit offers a real bonus for the consumer - a pouch in the cupboard to freshen up any one of countless dishes and at **any** time of the year.

## Flexibility and convenience

Because the mango is not an easy fruit to work with, the number of dishes it can be used in is rather restricted. But in pulp form it is perfect for mixing with the likes of: curries, cereals, yoghurt, rice, smoothies, milk shake, ice cream, cocktails and mocktails.

Also because of the difficulty in peeling a mango, much of the flesh is wasted. Whereas with the pouch, it is a case of open and mix in! The amount of wastage is greatly reduced, so consumers can enjoy more of the product.

### Price

One 200g pouch contains two whole mangoes. When the price is compared to buying two *Alphonso* mangoes in a supermarket, the price actually works out cheaper!

### Work in progress

As I said at the beginning of this section, at the time of writing, this is very much a 'work in progress' situation. However the good news is that now armed with the numerous 'why us' benefits that the company actually possess, they have successfully gained appointments with several major supermarket chains in the UK. Moreover the reception they have received from

*Mangoes are not easy to peel, although easier than this amateur is making out!*

buyers has been wholly more positive than at their first presentation.

If ever a product has earned the right to appear on a supermarket shelf in the UK, I believe it is this product. The people behind the company are genuine, dedicated people and they will have my continued support in their quest for success.

## 7.2 So, why YOU and why ME?!
*What is it that WE have that makes us feel we must introduce ourselves to our target customers?*

Now you've read 7.0 and 7.1 I'd like you to consider what **your** answer would be if I asked the question, *'Why you?'*

Please remember that it should be the one thing that makes you feel like knocking down doors down to introduce yourself to your target audience.

*Because **you know** you can benefit them!*

It means that you have considered everything that exists as an option to your offering and you **still** feel you have something unique that they should be aware of.

Write down everything on a piece of paper that you feel is special and sums up the unique DNA of your offering. Is it the price of your product or service, or the way you deliver it? Could it be a special feature you have added to enhance the offering, maybe a different type of service level, or guarantee? Is it your expertise or experiences in a particular field that makes you stand out?

Please know that I **also** have had to go through the very same exercise before producing this book, what is it that made **me** feel I simply had to introduce myself?

Am I in the top 10 marketing gurus in the world? **No,** I'm much better than **that!** I'm joking… well **sort** of joking!

I have completed somewhere between two and three thousand projects, across every market place imaginable. Do anything that number of times and you begin to become pretty good at it; you begin to understand the effects certain actions will have, the way consumers will react.

For 25 years I have done this day in day out on the very front line where as I said elsewhere in this book there are **no** hiding places, something either works or it doesn't and you find out pretty damn fast!

Over time this experience becomes *instinct* and I just love sharing this with the real heroes in business, the *start-ups* and *small enterprises.* As one of them, you are facing really difficult challenges and tough odds to overcome.

Yet you **can** do it, just remember the basics in this book and time and again test your offering against them. Make sure you never lose the understanding of what your brand represents and what it is that makes you special, unique and feeling that want to kick doors down to tell people.

Go on a **crusade,** to tell people **'why you!'**

If you need any more inspiration have a look at the last section in this chapter where even a **breakfast** can be the *'why you!'*

## 7.3 Vicar's Ruin...

### ...a devilishly good breakfast!

In this chapter we have so far examined case histories from as far apart as bollards to mangoes; both however with the common denominator of discovering what they **really** have to offer their target audiences.

By the end of it they were able to answer with confidence the key question, *"Why You?"*

I've decided to include this particular story, because it shows that often the key *'why you'* difference can actually be something quite small; but nonetheless popular with customers.

Having spent much of the past decade working across the county of Northumberland I have met many small businesses that are tourist related and indeed have included some in this book. This is another such example, from a small independent accommodation provider; a *bed and breakfast* that I visited several years ago.

I asked the lady owner the same key question I ask all small businesses, *'Why you?'* She explained that it was not easy to answer that as her B&B was not directly connected with any historic site, nor had it won any awards and so she felt there wasn't as such any real distinguishing feature she could build on.

She did however say that she kept a guest book for comments (which is a great idea that we'll speak about in 12.1). On reading through it was clear her guests were full of praise for the cleanliness of accommodation and warmth of welcome.

There was however one other feature that stood out, being mentioned in several testimonials - the **breakfast!**

She laughed and said that she always made a point of telling guests that while staying with her they would be treated to a **Northumbrian** breakfast, not an English one! "All our produce is local; eggs, bacon, sausages and even the mead!"

"Mead; for breakfast?" I asked with surprise, while actually being very interested; I might even come here for a stay I thought!

She explained that as with her other breakfast ingredients, it is locally made, on the Holy Island of Lindisfarne, fermented from honey, white grapes and herbs.

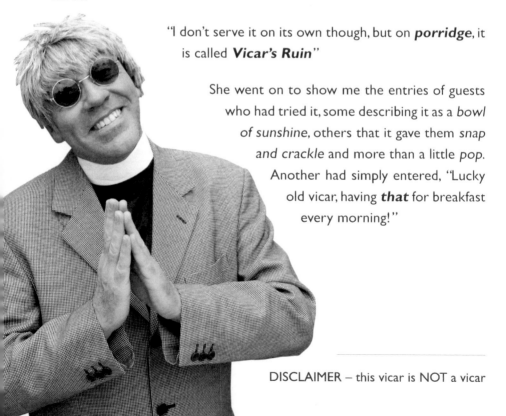

"I don't serve it on its own though, but on **porridge**, it is called **Vicar's Ruin**"

She went on to show me the entries of guests who had tried it, some describing it as a *bowl of sunshine*, others that it gave them *snap and crackle* and more than a little *pop*. Another had simply entered, "Lucky old vicar, having **that** for breakfast every morning!"

DISCLAIMER – this vicar is NOT a vicar

"It seems you have a hit on your hands here," I said. I think that you may also have a small *'Why me'*.

This proved to be the case as a few weeks later she called to tell me that she had been featured in a tourism article about Northumberland. She had immediately mentioned her *Vicar's Ruin* breakfast dish and they had written a splendid piece on it - what's more it **worked,** as she received around twenty direct enquiries from readers of the article.

So it just shows that it doesn't need to be some big investment to get a *'why you'*, sometimes experience of a market and a bit of imagination is all it takes.

Incidentally we return to the topic of alcohol at breakfast time in section 10.5, where I get my own chance to have an alcoholic start to the day…

More a case of…
**Marketing Man's Ruin!**

# CHAPTER 8

# HAS YOUR BRAND GOT THE RIGHT FORMULA?

### Find out by testing it on your target customers!

Many people decide to start their own small business because as a consumer they have looked to buy a product or service only to find it isn't available, or at least not in the format they want. They then see a possible business opportunity, a gap in the market and so move to fill it by offering it themselves.

In doing so they begin to formulate not only what they are going to do, but how… their *brand*.

Clearly they will need **others** like them, who will also want this offering and the way in which it is presented; are there enough of them, or is there a reason why this area of the market isn't populated, lack of demand for instance?

Believe it or not, many start-up business owners have **no** idea until they launch, because they didn't **ask!** Instead some scratch around in search engines and regard that as *market research* and *'job done!'*

In its simplest form market research is about defining your proposed offering and then validating it with those whose money you want!

The key part of that sentence is '*whose money you want*' in other words those you believe to be your **target audience**. Instead of that many start-up businesses settle for asking their friends and family!

Now that might be fair enough if your family and friends are truly representative of your core target audience, but often this isn't the case. The problem with just asking those closest, is that they may want to be supportive of you and your idea and therefore might not want to *pop your balloon* by saying what they really think. By trying to be loyal, they may in reality be doing you a disservice.

The next thing to be clear about is
what you are going to say to them
about your offering. You may begin
by explaining that you are looking
to introduce a new product or service
and you believe them to be typical of your
perceived target audience and give your reasons for this
assumption. As such you would welcome their feedback on what they
think of it and would they be likely to buy it if it were on the market? Now
as far as that goes, great - except that it **doesn't go far enough.**

There is one critical element missing, one word - **price!**

Without knowing what is it going to cost them how can anyone know for
sure whether they would buy it? There is an old saying that *'the only real
form of market research is ask people for their money!'*

Now that may be a little difficult until you are actually in business but what
you can at least do is say you are considering selling it for £x, then ask,
"Would **you** buy it for that?"

Or flip it on its head and invite those you are questioning to say what they
would be prepared to pay for it.

Then and only then will you begin to discover if you are on to a winner
or not. In fact occasionally people may surprise you by stating they would
be prepared to pay **more** for your offering than you had envisaged (see
section 8.3).

So please remember in market research, once you have formulated and costed your proposed product or service, question those who you believe to be most representative of your core *target audience* - and remember to include *'price'*.

Clearly this form of market research should be undertaken **prior** to finalising your offering and certainly before launching - and yet amazingly it often isn't. It is little wonder then that so many start-up businesses end up with a *Ready, Fire,* **AIM** situation.

## 8.1 Man you're nuts!
### *A stand-up's put down!*

As a celebratory launch for this book I had the idea of presenting an evening of stand-up comedy, linked to all areas of marketing. I hired a theatre venue and began to think about show content and presentation.

Although having given many talks on marketing I had never done anything like **this** before and thought it therefore wise to find out more about today's stand-up comedy scene (*market research!*).

While DVDs are all very well I wanted to sample the atmosphere of a live stand-up show and so went to a small theatre where an alternative comedian was playing - and boy **was** he alternative!

He appeared on stage as a cross-dressing Goth and somewhat disconcertingly was matched in dress code by a number of the audience. After the show which was actually very clever and funny, I decided to have a drink in the bar before heading home.

About 15 minutes later the comedian also came in with a couple of other people. Telling them to take a seat he came to the bar and ordered the drinks. Looking over I nodded and told him I'd just been to his show. He thanked me, but added, "You're not exactly typical of my normal audience demographic!"

I think the fact that I was not wearing a leather mini skirt and fishnets gave the game away - I had the wrong **branding!**

I then made a bad mistake! Stupidly I responded to his comment by stating that I had *'my own stand-up show'* going and that it was always good to learn from others, adding, "If you have any tips I'd be interested in hearing them." God what was I saying?!

He said for him he always begins a tour by playing the first few gigs in small venues, as it is hard to know if the material he's written will work until he tries in front of an audience.

Then he and his manager review reactions from these *work in progress* gigs before finalising show content for the next **hundred** or so dates.

He then turned to me and said, "So how many dates do you have on **your** tour?"

The question although I guess an obvious one totally took me by surprise and realising my mega mistake of making out I was the next *'big thing'* in comedy, gave the spluttered response of, "Erm… well, you know, just erm… well just… just the… **one.**"

The look on his face was perfectly matched by his words. Picking up his drinks, he turned and said, "Man you're **nuts,**" then walked off!

Of course he was right! **I** preach to others about market research and assessing your offering through the eyes of your target audience and here was **me** doing the exact opposite; believing my audience would like whatever I said with no way at all of knowing if that would be the case until the night.

Whereas he, by researching his comic offering to sample target audiences **before** the big tour was minimising the risk of failure - *makes sense doesn't it?*

That said I'm still not sure about the **fishnets,** no matter **what** my target audience say!

## 8.2 Your mind is like a parachute…

*…it won't work unless it's open*

One of the great difficulties in **you** undertaking your own market research is trying to remain impartial regarding both the questions you ask and interpretation of the results.

It is human nature to want people to agree with you and your concept and as this is also your dream, it is an especially sensitive area. Yet it is better to face disappointment at this stage, rather than after a full-scale, costly launch of your enterprise and potential public failure.

An American democratic politician once faced this consequence, being crushed in the primaries, by the voters who felt he hadn't listened to them. His concession speech however was brilliant, consisting of just one sentence, "The people have spoken… the **bastards!**"

Therefore no matter how tough it is, please listen carefully to your target audience **before** you decide to launch your enterprise. I'd suggest you either get someone else to conduct the research, or if you are to do it yourself then please do not **load** the questions in favour of your hoped-for response.

Besides, how much more satisfying it is if they **love** what you are proposing without you having to **lean** on them? What's more they may surprise you with their responses in that they may make a really significant suggestion you hadn't thought of and one which enhances your proposed offering.

Maybe revisit your model in the light of their comments and then go back and see them **again** with a revised offering and see what their response is now.

As this section header says, *'your mind is like a parachute, it won't work unless it's open,'* so please also be aware of receiving *buying signals* regarding any potential opportunities that may be voiced.

These openings can be missed through people not fully being open to what is being said by the target audience.

I remember many years ago when I was a fashion buyer in the retail trade, seeing one of the store's older sales assistants shaking her head while speaking with a young man in the shirt department.

After he'd left I approached and asked her why we couldn't help him. She shrugged and replied, "Why do people keep asking for black shirts, when **nobody** wants them!"

You see to her, at her advanced years, black shirts were the Devil's work, all *sex and rock 'n roll*. Her mind was closed to the possibility that people may just want black shirts as they were in fashion. Signals from the target audience were ignored and so sales were lost.

If **you** can open your mind and react to what your core target audience are telling you, the more **they** will open their wallets.

## 8.3 Say it with flowers...
*...sell at the right price and get a 'blooming' good profit margin*

Small business owners often believe that market research is only to be employed when first launching their enterprise; when in reality it is a key component at every stage of their growth.

Such was the situation with the small business in this case history. The company was a family-run florist in Yorkshire. They had just completed their third year in business when I visited them and their challenge was one of *profitability*.

From the sales they made, allowing for all outlays, salaries and running costs,

the net profit at the end of each year was around £500. That kind of surplus gave only a very small cushion should they encounter just one bad year.

The problem was that they couldn't increase the size of the shop and so generating additional sales was difficult. Even if they could increase turnover, their staffing level, already trimmed to a minimum, would struggle to service the additional workload.

I knew the best way out of the dilemma was to increase prices and therefore margins, while holding overheads at the same or similar level. As I surveyed the shop my eye was drawn to six completed floral displays awaiting collection by the delivery driver.

"Do you mind if I ask your customers some questions?" The owner agreed and I quickly drew a matrix on a piece of paper; the numbers 1-6 along the top for the six floral arrangements and then a grid of empty boxes to enter prices in underneath.

Over the next hour before they were collected by the delivery driver, I asked every customer who came into the shop for their opinion about how much they thought each floral arrangement would cost. I duly noted the figures that each visitor gave me under the appropriate display.

Before the arrangements disappeared with the driver, I asked the owner how much each **actually** cost and I entered these prices at the top of each display's column.

Together we then compared them and the effect on the owner was profound. Out of around 15 people questioned almost every single response across the six arrangements showed well above the actual price they were sold for. Overwhelmingly consumers were valuing the shop's offering at higher that the prices charged.

The owner whist being surprised at the actual research felt that she couldn't raise prices significantly. She explained that a main part of the reason that people perceived them so high was the **presentation.** She had spent two years working in a Parisian flower shop, where presentation is an art form. When she moved to the UK with her husband she maintained her French supplier connections and shipped in bulk the same presentation supplies.

At this point I suggested that if she felt unable to raise prices across the board that she at least consider one other suggestion. I proposed that each day she make up two identical floral arrangements, (in terms of flowers used), but present one in the way other UK florists do and the second in the Parisian style that had so impressed those I had spoken with.

At the point of a customer placing their order the shop's staff would then show them the two options of presentation.

I suggested she make a small (£1.00) additional charge for the Parisian presentation, although the materials were almost identical in terms of cost. This gave customers only a £1.00 decision to make for something which had a much greater perceived value.

She agreed to this and at the end of the following year she had just over 2,000 customers out of around 3,700 annual transactions who opted for the £1.00 extra.

As the cost of implementing this change was virtually nil, the additional profit generated went straight on the bottom line.

This resulted in the equivalent of **4 years profit in 12 months, without spending a penny extra on advertising!**

Now of course not every business has this kind of opportunity; that said I would like to issue you with the following challenge. Is there anything in your business where you could offer either a deluxe, premium or a fast-track option at a higher price?

The key is to do so without dramatically adding to your overheads; that way the additional income goes straight on the bottom line profit.

## 8.4 Onward and upward...

### ...continue to listen, continue to grow

Before leaving this chapter please remember that market research can be used not only to test the market for new products or services, but also to **evaluate** current performance from **existing customers.**

We will speak later in this book about the importance of valuing current clients, but in this section I would draw your attention to a **great** way of knowing what your customers think of your service.

The example shown here is used by a tourism attraction with refreshment facilities and I have a number of other clients in different markets who use something very similar to evaluate the satisfaction levels of their customers.

The problem not just with this type of visitor attraction, but many other types of business, is that customers often do not let the company itself know of any dissatisfaction on their part, but instead - and even worse -

they let their friends and acquaintances know. In this way often the very last person to find out there is a problem is the actual business owner and by then much damage to reputation may have been done.

So my suggestion to every one of my clients and of course to **you**, is that no matter the nature or size of your enterprise, please proactively seek the opinions of your customers.

In this case I suggested to my client that he introduce a postcard that visitors would be invited to complete on their exit from the attraction; while their feelings were very fresh.

The postcard asked for satisfaction levels across a number of criteria to be scored out of 10, where I represents complete dissatisfaction and 10 denotes maximum satisfaction.

The card takes only a couple of minutes to complete and provides the owner with an up to date evaluation of their offering, as seen through the eyes of the people who are paying for it, their customers.

*Help us grow...*

by giving us some
feedback on your visit

What's more if the exercise is **continued** on an on-going basis it will provide the business with a satisfaction indicator, in other words a benchmark against which to compare future performance.

For example if on average the refreshment facilities score over 90% satisfaction rating over the course of a year and then suddenly in the 13th month fall dramatically to around 40%, clearly something has happened to cause such a blip. This could perhaps be a menu change, or perhaps price increase, change of décor and so on.

The point I'm making is that this type of market research acts as an **early warning system** that something has changed and for the worse. Conversely if a new innovation or improvement has been introduced then the cards are an excellent way to record and compare any significant increase in satisfaction.

It is true that this takes a little time to set up and evaluate - but **only** a little and when this is compared to the benefits it will generate, it is time very well spent. Please remember just like a puppy, *market research* is for life.

Continue to **listen,** continue to **act** and you will continue to **grow.**

# CHAPTER 9

# THE SHOCKING ALTERNATIVE (AND NEARLY TRUE) HISTORY OF THE KILT!

*The few words by which you stand or fall*

Now that you have worked out what position you occupy in your chosen market place, defined what your *brand* is and had your offering corroborated by your *target audience*, what next?

Another challenge, that's what! I'd now like you to sum up your *brand* in just a few words. I know that on the face of it this probably seems an odd or even wasteful use of your time, so let me first of all explain why this is so important **and** throw in an impromptu and almost accurate, history lesson too!

So first of all what to call these few words? Many people will refer to them as a *'slogan'*, others a *'strap-line'*, or *'tag-line'*, some will even go for the grander sounding *'mission statement'*.

Actually these terms differ in meaning from each other, but in reality I don't mind so much what you call these few words, just as long as you know their importance for your business.

For me, I want them to give **life** to your business; **heralding** your *brand*

That's quite a bit to pack in to just a few words; which is why **I** refer to them as your **brand promise.** They are the commitment by which your business will stand or fall.

Last year I spoke at an international business conference in Geneva on this very subject. A member of the audience commented that these types of *mission statements* were not new, but originated in America back in the early 70's. He went on to say that you still see them in large organisations, A4 in size, framed and hung in reception areas.

> ### Mission Statement
>
> *We commit to serve our customers with diligence and civility, thereby strengthening the valued bond that will enable us to build a platform toward greater partnership, mutual understanding, trust and benefit.*
>
> *Our knowledge and professionalism will combine to problem-solve for our clients, as part of a company culture of superior customer service.*
>
> *We aim to achieve profitable growth, through innovation and quality.*
>
> *We will be guided through the marketplace by a relentless focus on operational excellence in every corner of our organisation.*
>
> *Through investment in our core values we aim to meet or exceed our commitments and our longer-term strategic planning will be shaped by a set of central ideals that are spurred by market demands and the critical imperatives necessary to achieve our vision.*

The example above is the kind of framed statement he was referring to; please have a read through it.

Are you still awake? You **are**; I'm impressed! Especially as none of the above gives any **real** indication of what this company actually does! I guarantee that no one will remember a fraction of what it says and it could apply to almost any organisation.

What's more how exactly do you **use** it, when no one, customers nor staff will remember any of it?

Even though it is full of fine sounding sentiments, there is a much better way to let potential customers know what you do and *'why you'* **and** that can be said in no more than just a few words; sometimes just **one!**

A number of years ago I learned at first hand that these longer mission statements were ineffective. I had been dealing with the director of a large enterprise and after presenting my proposal to him for a marketing project, he felt sufficiently impressed to take matters to the final step, a meeting with the *chief executive*.

During this second meeting I explained what I meant by a *brand promise* and as I was doing so the *chief executive* interjected, pointing to an A4 frame containing his company's *mission statement* that was sitting on his desk. He went on to describe how he had insisted these were placed on the desk of each director, so that daily they could come face-to-face with their company's mission.

I said that whilst admiring this thinking would he mind if I asked him something? He gave me the *green light* to do so, at which point I leaned forward and placed the A4 frame containing the *mission statement* face down on the desk.

"Can you tell me exactly what your mission statement that you come face-to-face with daily says?" Looking somewhat agitated he stammered, "Well there's a bit about our customers."

"Great!" I said, "That's **one** word!"

At this point, failing to add to this, he gave one of the best bits of delegation, or blame shifting, I've ever witnessed. Nodding toward the director I'd previously met he said, "**You** tell John, after all you were more involved with putting it together in the first place."

It was hard not to smile when I saw the look on his fellow director's face, because from when I had been in his office, **his** A4 framed statement was covered with post-it notes; he used it as a **noticeboard!**

So you can see why such statements really don't work. Now before moving on to what **does** work I'd like to give the promised 'almost accurate' history lesson.

You see mission statements, strap-lines, slogans or call them what you will, did **not** originate in America in the 70s. Instead they came from where all good things in this world come... **Scotland!**

It's true, if you think of it we have given the world the **television,** the **telephone,** the game of **golf** and of course **whisky**... yes, we gave the world **party time!**

Can you imagine the *Research and Development* department of the Scottish whisky industry back in *fifteen oatcake* when they realised just what they had **and** on their very doorstep?! Oh my word, what an era to live in; as a nation I think we were sozzled for half a century and when we finally sobered up guess what we found... we were wearing our *wives'* kit!!

"How did **this** happen and more to the point how are we going to save our reputation for being fearsome warriors when we're all wearing skirts?!"

Then someone had a stroke of marketing genius, "I know, let's call it our **national costume.**"

**Brilliant!** And that is **my** take on how our national costume came into being. It's true that the history books will tell you something completely different - but I'm the marketing man here, so **you** decide!

But in addition to all the good things my nation has given this world, we have also contributed to short mission statements; they were in fact called **mottos** and each family or Clan had one.

These were precious values by which the Clan would live and even die. And they didn't run into battle carrying an A4 framed, 200 word mission statement, shouting, "We promise to decapitate, maim and seriously damage you, but with due care and attention, within budget and with one eye on sustainability!"

There was none of that, instead just the one, two or three words that summed up what their Clan stood for, their beliefs, in a sense their *brand*.

When **you** go onto the business battlefield you will also need your *motto* or *brand promise* to inspire and spur you on! These few words cost nothing, yet mean **everything.** They are the few words that drive all that you do.

Like the Scottish clans you are also very courageous entering into battle every day, often against the odds with everything on the line.

So now it is important for you to **hoist your own standard,** one that sums up the **heart** of your business. Use it as your banner, your guide and your motivation; it is after all **your** *raison d'être*, your reason for being.

## 9.1 Your brand...
### ...your **promise**

When considering what your *brand promise* might be please try and focus on the key elements of your offering, your *'why you'* unique qualities.

Try also to stay away from the *superlatives trap*. You wouldn't believe the number of times I've had clients say they were thinking of having, *'Simply the best'* for their *brand promise*. Being a new enterprise with no established track record means this simply isn't credible.

Likewise when I see the word *'quality'*, what is that based on? If they have won awards for *quality* then fine, but otherwise it is nearly meaningless. It's the same with expressions like, *'affordable prices'*. My question would immediately be, "*affordable for* **whom?**"

In my consultancy business, for many years I had the brand promise of, **'Seeing your business through different eyes.'** I based this on the fact that over 20 years of visiting hundreds of businesses on the *front line*, I had accumulated a myriad of experiences, both good and bad, from which to draw on.

Therefore when I was invited to view a new client's offering, I genuinely was adding something different that would be hard for them to get elsewhere. I **really was** able to view their enterprise through *different eyes* and this was of real value to them.

For this book too, I again had to decide on the *brand promise* with which to spearhead its entry into the marketplace. When researching the market for books on the topic of *marketing*, I encountered a great many, but nearly all were what I would describe as 'text books' and many of them a pretty heavy going read.

So I decided that my brand would be a new concept, one based on my own practical experiences, a book that would be easy to read **and** a bit of fun, aimed almost exclusively at start-up and small business owners.

The 'fun' part is not in any way meant to trivialise the subject, just to make it a more accessible read. If I succeed in achieving this, the likelihood of readers actually finishing the book will be increased! I am passionate about small businesses beating the odds and becoming a success and I believe the advice in this book really can help. My *brand promise* therefore is:

*Putting the* **'smile of success'** *into small business.*

## 9.2 From the perfect cappuccino...
### ...to a 6' 4" fantasy actress

Now for some examples of *brand promises* I've worked on with clients, all in very different market places.

Each of these sums up in just a few words what that company, their product or service **promises to deliver.** These are the key words that drive their business, the very foundation of their enterprise.

I've included some notes about why in the following examples I felt that the few words chosen were appropriate in summing up their *brand promise*.

My sincere thanks goes to each of the following named companies for kindly allowing their example to be shown here, in the hope that it may benefit others.

**The heart of a great coffee**

Like most people I enjoy a good coffee when in town… well at least up until the hour when it is deemed decent to switch to a glass of wine!

There are plenty of coffee shops to choose from nowadays and although the large international chains dominate the high street, for me there is nothing better than discovering a small gem of an Italian cafe, that serves authentic espresso or cappuccino.

Indeed some even employ their very own 'barista', an Italian word for someone who is an expert in making perfect espresso and espresso based drinks. Order a cappuccino in my favourite coffee shop and the barista will serve it complete with latte art!

Of course to do this you need to be an experienced hand in the critical skill of attaining the correct texture of the milk - essential for the perfect latte or cappuccino. Until now, unless you have this skill, making the perfect coffee remains in the province of the baristas.

However thanks to one of my clients that has all changed, because now we - yes even **me** - can make the perfect cappuccino **and** every time too!

Graeme Stewart of *Milk to Perfection* is a former barista himself and he has developed an innovative product, a jug that spins the milk automatically as it heats. With the correct milk texture you get the perfect result.

The *brand promise* Graeme and I agreed best summed up his offering was, **'The heart of a great coffee'**. We reinforced this by showing a latte art heart in his branding.

I'll leave you to check the rest of the product details out on his website (www.milktoperfection.co.uk), but suffice to say that it **works;** I tried it myself and can now actually make the perfect cappuccino - *so how come I'm still single?*

**For a smoother check-in**

I never ceased to be amazed by the ingenuity and determination of entrepreneurs.

This next example begins with a frustrated businessman standing in a long airline check-in queue where there was a hold up due to one of the passengers luggage being in excess of the permitted allowance.

The offending passenger's embarrassment and frustration spilled over into anger when he was given the ultimatum by the member of check-in staff to either remove items from his case or pay excess charges, which came to over £50.

As the businessman stood there witnessing this he realised that this was a 'lose-lose' situation for everyone. Passengers in the queue were inconvenienced by the delay; the offending passenger had lost his temper taking his frustration out on the check-in operator who was just doing her job, even the airport itself could well lose income the passenger may have otherwise spent in the retail outlets had his money not had to go to pay excess charges.

Worse still, if the passenger decided not to pay the excess and instead dump items from his baggage in the terminal, this could have the potential of sparking a security alert, causing delays for everyone.

The businessman who witnessed and considered all this was Gerard Stewart and together with his wife Carole and later other family members Graeme and Marc formed a company called *Weigh-ahead* to solve the problem of excess baggage at airport check-in desks, so that a more positive environment for everyone involved would be achieved.

They went on to develop a very sophisticated pre check-in luggage weighing system for airline passengers to use **before** reaching the desk. In this way passengers can verify if their luggage is overweight and if so what the likely excess charges will be.

Then they can calmly assess the situation without delaying others and come to an informed choice as to what to do prior to checking in. Indeed Gerard and Carole even had the brainwave of installing a vending machine selling their own brand of cabin-compliant foldaway 'smart bags'; thereby offering a potential solution to the problem by allowing passengers to transfer items from their case to the bag.

Since then *Weigh-ahead* have picked up a number of impressive business awards in recognition of their advanced weighing systems which even update with airline information in real time. *Weigh-ahead* systems can be seen today in major airports across the world, benefitting daily thousands of passengers.

The *brand promise* that encompasses their drive and objective harks back to the day that Gerard and Carole stood in that long queue waiting for his flight, **'For a smoother check-in.'**

## Packing your reputation

Contract packing, or product manipulation to give it its Sunday name, is a demanding and competitive business. The service involves the presentation of top branded products, so they look their very best.

Around 10 years ago I met Judith Leighton managing director of *Assembly and Packaging Services (APS)* in Blyth. Since then *APS* has grown into one of the UK's largest contract packing organisations, servicing the complex needs of many blue chip clients, across numerous high street brands.

Their varied services include: repackaging, relabelling, shrink wrap packaging, multiple product banding & sleeving. Indeed such is the trust the company enjoys from some of the high street's best known proprietary products, that they now offer a complete service from design and procurement, through to manipulation and on to storage and distribution.

When considering the *brand promise* of the company I was struck by Judith's total commitment to ensuring her clients received the very best service. She told me that the next time many of the products *APS* handle would be seen is on a supermarket shelf and if there should be any mistake it would reflect badly on the standing of the product in the eyes of consumers.

Judith demonstrates her total commitment to a premium service by conducting quality checks at each stage of the *APS* process. Her mission is to aim for perfection, so that the reputation of her clients and their proprietary products will be enhanced from the association they have had with *APS*.

In proposing the *brand promise* I took my lead from Judith, offering just three words, that sum up her recognition of the trust her clients place in *APS*, **'Packing your reputation'.**

I renewed my acquaintance with Judith recently and was delighted to hear that these three words still drive her and all that *APS* do.

## Just right!

Sometimes even when other companies have identical products to your own, you can still offer something different, **something better.** Such was the case in this next example, a family run business involved in the supply, installation and servicing of refrigeration units for retail food outlets.

The owners had asked me to undertake a branding exercise and during the course of this I asked them the question (well you *knew* I would) 'why you?'

Normally when I ask this I get responses that can be a little vague, but not on this occasion. The owner explained that if a company such as his really wanted to demonstrate a 'duty of care' to customers, then this would carry through **past** the point of sale.

I immediately jumped in, "You are referring of course to servicing if something goes wrong with one of your units?" His reply took me a little by surprise, "**Before** servicing, I'm referring to installation!"

What he then said **really** impressed me, which is why all these years later I recall it.

He explained that the real cost of refrigerated units is not just the selling price, but the **running costs**. If the temperature of a unit is set too high the food is in danger, but if set too low then the electricity costs are higher than need be and this over the course of a year can be a very substantial and avoidable cost. He showed me figures to demonstrate this, showing that even just a small misalignment could prove really costly.

His 'why me' factor centred on the fact that he surveyed each area that a unit was situated in at the point of installation. After considering a number factors he then gave his customer recommended seasonal settings that would allow the unit to run at optimal efficiency, safeguarding food, and saving money.

The two word *brand promise* I gave him reflected this attention to detail, not too hot, not too cold, **'Just right.'**

## A cinematic approach

# big river
# FILMS

I have had for a number of years the very real pleasure of being a guest lecturer and mentor at two great universities, *Newcastle University* and the *University of Northumbria*.

There is something so special about meeting really fresh, creative talent that these universities produce. One such person I met a couple of years ago was Alastair Cummings who together with his business partner Richard Power run *Big River Films*.

They describe themselves as: 'a *video production company focused on creating innovative music videos, attention grabbing documentaries and engaging corporate videos*', all of which is true.

However they missed one key element out in that statement - they **love** to make movies! Every video they make is a film! Even corporate videos in their hands have a cinematic twist to them.

They have a knack of engaging audiences through film and so for me it was a very easy choice to suggest the three word *brand promise* of, '**A cinematic approach.**'

Incidentally, I have recently worked with *Big River Films* on some short marketing films of my own to be shown on my website and YouTube - and can I just say to any ladies reading this that I believe you'll find that I look pretty cool in them, a sort of Celtic George Clooney I think (in the interests of editorial balance here, I should point out that those who have seen the films are still laughing at this comparison... but as I've told them, jealousy is a terrible affliction).

**Keeping you on course**

A number of years ago I undertook a project for a company who offered a floating ship repair service, a little like a marine version of the AA, or RAC.

This 'afloat' repairs and maintenance service was for all types and sizes of marine vessels across the commercial sectors, ranging from small fishing boats to larger bulk carriers and tankers.

The key element of their service was that they would go to a stricken vessel, thereby saving a costly detour to the nearest port. By helping to keep them on schedule in this way, financial penalties and expensive repair stop-overs were therefore avoided.

The four word *brand promise* I suggested to my client perfectly summed up their business mission, **'Keeping you on course.'**

### Introducing Dixie!

This last *brand promise* example is NOT one of mine and even though quite distasteful in some ways it is nevertheless quite brilliant in others **and** it does go to illustrate that every industry can use the marketing principles as set out in this book.

After finishing some paperwork late one evening, I decided to see if there were any 'late night documentaries'... on channel 5 (well I am a **single!**) - and guess what, there was!

The main premise of this 'adult entertainment' documentary was to chart the 'going-ons' at what I believe was called a *'Chicken Ranch'* in America – and I'm not talking clucking poultry here either!

I seem to remember that to make the situation even more bizarre, the 'clients' were actually flown in by plane to a small landing strip! From there they were escorted inside and made comfortable while the ladies of the house, or fantasy actresses, introduced themselves and gave their 'why me' *brand promises*.

For the purposes of the documentary the camera played the role of the client and each girl came and spoke directly into it, winking and pouting as they did so. It was at this point that one girl gave what quite possibly is the best *brand promise* I ever heard!

She went by the name of Dixie, I'm sure that was her real name. As she slinked toward the camera she looked to be one of the tallest girls I think I've ever seen. What followed was pure gold.

Looking straight down the barrel of the camera she delivered the following *brand promise*, "I'm 6' 4" and worth the climb." Then with a wink she whispered, "And if you get tired you can stop half way up!"

Genius!

If I live to be 100 I'll never produce a *brand promise* to top **that!**

**Photograph:** The part of Dixie was superbly modelled for this book by Laura Jane Carson (who has NEVER been to a chicken ranch!!)

## 9.3 Plug your brand promise...

*...into **all** that you do*

To conclude this chapter on your company's *brand promise*, I would like to emphasise that it is not enough to just **have it,** it is imperative that you **live it!**

Plug it into every aspect of your business and demonstrate its relevance to your target customers. I would like to give you one example of doing this from my client casebook.

Several years ago I was invited to review the marketing of *Blyth Valley Borough Council* in Northumberland. In particular to highlight its mission to improve the quality of life for the population it served.

I spent some time visiting the area and in particular speaking with the *target audience*, those who lived there. In conclusion I gave them a single word *brand promise* to drive all their efforts,

# *'Pride.'*

I based this on the deep sense of *pride* those I encountered felt for their area. I then set about applying this to all aspects of the council's services, by quite literally plugging their *brand promise* into every area of work in which they were involved.

It was then branded on vehicles and literature pertaining to each service, as follows:

- *Pride, in our streets*
- *Pride, in our parks*
- *Pride, in our beaches*
- *Pride, in our schools*
- *Pride, in our people*

By plugging it in to every aspect of their business they were literally **living** their *brand promise*. Although in 2009 *Northumberland County Council* became a unitary authority and the council of Blyth Valley was abolished, the **Pride** that people have in in their area lives on.

# CHAPTER 10

# A SAINT AND A SINNER

*LEAD with your brand promise and stand out from the rest*

Once you have your *brand promise* the key thing then is to **lead** with it in all your communications. This is however something that small to medium size enterprises find very hard to do and in fact most don't!

Regarding your own enterprise, you will undoubtedly have much pride in the trading name you have chosen. It may be your family name or the result of months of searching, looking for that spark of inspiration.

Therefore when you first see your enterprise's name on your stationery, or at the top of an advertisement, it will feel like seeing your name up in lights, a terrific feeling! But that is *terrific for* **you**, not necessarily for your target audience who have no emotional buy-in to your trading name, or the story behind its development.

For them it is your **offering** that they are interested in! As a small business your advertising budget will be limited and so it is vital that you maximise every opportunity to *connect* your *brand* with your *target audience*.

Your trading name, especially when new, is hardly likely to achieve this, whereas your *why you* offering may well do. This chapter is therefore about using your *brand promise* and *why you* unique benefits, to help you **stand out from the crowd** and be noticed by your potential customers.

Although these examples are different, it is the principles behind each I'd like you to consider in your own offering for this type of **stand-out** treatment.

This chapter begins in section 10.1 with a story connected to a **saint** and ends in 10.5, with an example of how leading with a *brand promise* got one **sinner** into trouble at a *Jack Daniels* breakfast!

## 10.1 St Cuthbert passed our front door...
### ...don't you!

Sometimes **leading** with a key 'why you' feature can be the deciding factor in winning business. This next example is a case in point.

*Hazelrigg Bed and Breakfast* in Chatton, is situated between the breathtaking coastline of north Northumberland and the Cheviot Hills, a definite case of a *room with a view*, with glorious vistas on all sides.

The B&B, formerly a school, provides guests with accommodation that is modern, comfortable and with a bit of character. One look at their guestbook and it is clear that this combination is a winning one, with many saying their stay was a real highpoint in their visit to Northumberland.

Little touches like welcoming guests, many who have travelled long distances, with a cup of tea, or glass of wine and slice of cake (real nice cake too!), are appreciated and remembered.

With so much going for their B&B, why had the owners invited me in to help with their marketing? The challenge they explained was tipping the balance in their favour with visitors who were planning where to stay during their visit to north Northumberland.

Many of the facilities they offer sound similar to other accommodation providers and they just felt they would like more of a cutting edge with which to lead their marketing efforts, in particular on their website and in advertising.

My first thought was to perhaps build something around the fact their property was a school, but we all felt that was not the 'big hit' they were looking for. I then noticed some home-made literature that they had produced on their computer. It contained a list of what to see in the area as well as a short history. One name interested me, that of 'St Cuthbert.'

I remembered from a dim and distant history lesson that he was a 7th century saint, who had embarked on a famous walk from Melrose in the Scottish borders to Holy Island off the Northumberland coast.

"Did his walk come close to where the B&B is?" I enquired. "Right past the front door," was the reply, "we are **on** St Cuthbert's Way"

That was the factor they were seeking and within 24 hours Hazelrigg's website headline became, *'St Cuthbert passed our front door,* **don't you!***'*

Since then the ratio of website visitors to hard enquiries has risen quite sharply. Many of those who book said the headline had caught their eye and was an added attraction, staying somewhere that such an historic figure had been near.

Others said it just made them smile (and we know that smiling is good!) which made them stay on the website longer, looking through the accommodation facilities. An analysis of their website activity, confirmed that since the headline had changed visitors were indeed staying longer on the site, indicating their positive interest.

It was simply people reacting to a headline that offered something *extra unusual* or *unique*. Although these examples relate to tourism (big in my part of the world), the same principle applies to other market places. Remember it is sometimes the small things that tip the balance in your favour.

There is so much communication *'noise'* today; we are all bombarded with marketing messages from every imaginable source. Therefore it is important to find a simple way of standing out from the crowd, a way that stops people in their tracks long enough to consider your offering.

Leading with your *brand promise* is one proven method of achieving this - and what's more it is FREE to implement.

## 10.2 Beautiful gardens...

### ...and a Prime Minister's famous cup of tea!

I have received the kind permission to share with you the following example of how leading with a *brand promise* and *'why you'* benefits can make a successful connection with a target audience.

*Howick Hall Gardens* in Northumberland are a garden lover's paradise. Their season starts in early February with a *'Snowdrop Festival'*, followed in late March and early April with spectacular drifts of daffodils throughout the grounds. In April and May their *Woodland Garden* offers a wonderful show of rhododendrons, camellias and magnolias. Also in May, the wildflower meadows are filled with beautiful tulips.

The formal gardens, including the herbaceous borders and terraces in front of the Hall, come into their own from June onwards. Year-round these gardens and extensive woodland walks have something to offer both tourist and local communities alike.

When I met the team at Howick they were reviewing their advertising for the following season's tourism publications. In previous years this had consisted of the heading, *'Howick Hall Gardens'* followed by a brief description of the gardens, woodland walks and tea house. You would imagine that with such wonderful gardens and arboretum that this offering was pretty much complete... but there was more!

For *Howick Hall* was also home of the Grey family from 1319, with *Charles 2nd Earl Grey* being the most distinguished member. As leader of the *Whig Party* he was *Prime Minister* from 1830 to 1834, during which time the *Great Reform Bill* of 1832 was passed in the teeth of opposition from the *Duke of Wellington*; this started the process of parliamentary reform which eventually led to our modern democracy. An amazing story!

As if this wasn't enough *Howick Hall* is also the home of the world famous *Earl Grey **tea!*** The tea was specially blended by a Chinese mandarin for *Charles, 2nd Earl Grey,* to suit the water from the well at Howick, using bergamot in particular, to offset the taste of the lime in it. *Lady Grey* used it in London when entertaining as a political hostess!

I placed myself in the position of the garden's main target audience, *tourists*. In doing so I felt that such a beautiful attraction with the **added** bonus of having once been where a *prime minister* had lived and where *Earl Grey tea* was born, would give me even greater impetus to visit. Therefore while leaving the advertisement size as before, we amended the header to read, '*Beautiful gardens, a Prime Minister and a famous cup of tea!*'

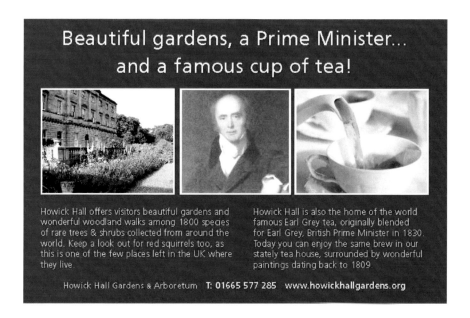

Beautiful gardens, a Prime Minister...
and a famous cup of tea!

Howick Hall offers visitors beautiful gardens and wonderful woodland walks among 1800 species of rare trees & shrubs collected from around the world. Keep a look out for red squirrels too, as this is one of the few places left in the UK where they live.

Howick Hall is also the home of the world famous Earl Grey tea, originally blended for Earl Grey, British Prime Minister in 1830. Today you can enjoy the same brew in our stately tea house, surrounded by wonderful paintings dating back to 1809.

Howick Hall Gardens & Arboretum   **T: 01665 577 285**   www.howickhallgardens.org

## 10.3 Want to ski?
### *Speak to me!*

There is one man I know who quite literally leads with his *brand promise* - in fact he **wears** it every day!

*Ski Reg*, as he is known to everyone, is one of the world's most knowledgeable and successful water ski instructors, he is also the most natural life coach I've ever met, the biggest character and my friend.

He is also known as *'the king of skis'* by those locals who witness him mono-ski at incredible speed off the coast of Costa Adeje, with his wife Mary at the wheel.

When Reg started in business on the island of Tenerife in the Canary Islands, he couldn't afford to drive around in a branded vehicle announcing his one-to-one water ski tuition service, so instead he invested in a couple of t-shirts and became a human 'advertising trailer'.

Emblazoned with the words, *'If you want to ski, speak to me'* his t-shirts are unmissable - much like Reg. But here's the thing, people **really do** speak with him and sign-up for skiing lessons. In fact he has built his business on this one form of marketing, plus the fact he is amazingly good at what he does.

In fact he was recently featured on Channel 5's *Rough Guide on Tenerife*, where he taught presenter Julia Bradbury to water ski - first time!

Indeed Reg has a success rate of over 90% with all first time skiers, leading to another one of his *brand promises* which goes, *'If I can't get you up first time, no one can!'* Hope he doesn't put **that** on his t-shirt!

### 10.4 Shifting your nuts…
*A 'tail' of a squirrel on the move!*

Who says business can't be fun?! Because every now and then it can be **great** fun!

One such occasion came with a branding enquiry from a new van hire company. I was asked by the client to research the local van hire market and come back with my thoughts and recommendations.

What I found was a succession of *'rent them cheap'* local companies, all of whom sounded and looked very similar. Choosing one would almost certainly be done by consumers trawling through online search engines, the Yellow Pages or local paper, checking for prices and availability.

Following some audience research it became clear that the majority of those renting were at the younger end of the spectrum, below 30. Mainly this involved moving their possessions from one property to another.

As the name of the company had already been decided, *Acorn Van Hire*, to match other companies in the same group, my mind moved to all things connected with acorns.

It wasn't long until the thought of squirrels came to mind - and where you have squirrels, nuts are not far behind - you can see where my mind was heading can't you?!

I have to say how much I admired the client's nerve; for when I presented the proposed van branding to him, he took a deep breath, laughed and then asked how soon I could do it!

He wasn't of course the only person to laugh! The first van caused quite a stir, raising more than a few smiles with the words *'Move your nuts with us'* emblazoned on the side and a giant squirrel's tail bringing up the rear… if you get my meaning!

When people smile it is a good sign and within literally a few days his van was the talk of the town and he had become the best known hire company in the area.

I did however prepare for the possibility that someone might complain and so contingencies were readied; happily these were never needed - but if you ever meet me ask about the **squirrel suit!**

## 10.5 A never to be forgotten Jack Daniels...
### ...breakfast!

This last example of leading with your *brand promise* to catch the attention of a target audience worked a treat - I should know as *I* was the target audience! Although I don't exactly cover myself in glory, this example does nevertheless sum up much of what is in this book.

You will remember in chapter 6, the case of the funeral companies, where two enterprises can be in the **same** sector, offering essentially the **same** service, in the **same** geographic area and even at the **same** price - and yet have two entirely **different** ways of doing it; **different** brands, aimed at **different** target customers. This is also the situation with this example.

I had to visit the *USA* on business. As such I was a consumer, with freedom of choice, looking to give my custom to a preferred accommodation provider.

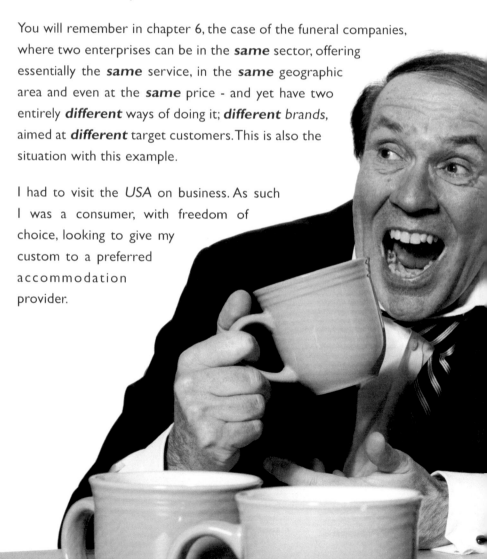

Although technically every single hotel in the state I was visiting was a potential target for my business, in reality this wasn't the case.

First of all the state I was visiting was pretty big and so I looked for somewhere close to where my business meeting was. This geographic zoning reduced dramatically the number of potential places to stay. Then came *cost* - my budget wasn't in the five star bracket, nor did I want one or two star. Next as I was *driving* I wanted secure overnight parking. In a sense I was segmenting the market until I found somewhere that was in the right geographic location, in the right price band, with the right facilities.

When I had zoned-in sufficiently, using this search criteria, my decision as to which of the remaining options to go with came down to a matter of personal taste.

As it turned out there were two prime candidates when I had drilled down in this way; one from memory was called, 'The Apple Blossom Inn'. From the advertisement it appeared to be a rather quaint establishment; the bedroom featured in the ad was lilac in colour with bowls of lavender potpourri and lace bed covers. It even offered a, 'welcoming refreshing cup of English tea on arrival'.

The other contender for my business didn't even mention its name in the advertisement header, instead choosing to lead with its *brand promise* which definitely succeeded in grabbing my attention,

**'Speciality of the house, Jack Daniels breakfasts'.**

Now as described earlier in this book (7.3) I'd previously come across *Lindisfarne Mead* with porridge *(Vicar's Ruin)* as a novel way of starting the day; but this seemed to take alcoholic breakfasts into a whole new dimension. I **love** *Jack Daniels* and so was *sold,* progressing from *consumer* to *customer!*

And so a week or so later I found myself entering the breakfast room I had seen featured in the advertisement. It was a little after 7.30 in the morning and I was looking forward to experiencing a different start to the day from my normal routine, the strongest element of which is a double espresso.

The hotel kept the *JD hype* going, emphasising on the special breakfast menu that it was only for those who were NOT driving, *'As we encourage responsible breakfast eating when motoring!'*

*Only in America,* I thought would you get a build-up for breakfast like **that!** When the waiter took my order he seemed delighted that I was, *'going Jack's way to start the day'* - god do they **ever** let up!

I followed his recommendation and chose pancakes and *Jack Daniels* syrup to begin. Now if we were going to do this dish in the UK, we'd probably add a soupçon of alcohol, **not** them, this was the full volume on a plate.

Just one mouthful and I realised my mistake. It was so strong that I thought my gums were going to melt! But I couldn't admit defeat and say it was too much for me, I am a **Scotsman** after all; and we **invented** whisky! So I struggled on, my cheeks turning a deep shade of red (approximately Pantone colour 186 C, for those with a design bent).

By the time the waiter collected my plate, my rosy red cheeks resembled that of a carol singer on a cold winter's evening. My tie too was by now undone and the highway to a town called 'Disgrace' was rapidly opening up in front of me!

My next mistake was opting for slices of toast thickly covered in Jack Daniels marmalade. This was matched in equal measure **and** equal folly by my decision to wash it all down with not one, not two, but three mugs of Jack Daniels coffee (well I assume there was coffee in the mugs, all I could taste was Jack).

By now I couldn't feel anything let alone **taste** anything, my mouth was numb, my taste buds paralytic… and my brain not far behind.

Worse still, I had morphed from a quiet, respectable businessman into the celebrity of the breakfast room! As people entered, I would give them the hale and hearty greeting of, "**HELLO!** My name is John, I'm from **Scotland!** I'm having a **Jack** breakfast… **YOU** should have a Jack breakfast too - let's **all** have a Jack breakfast!"

The problems didn't end there either, for when I'd finally finished and went to stand up to go, although my upper body was fully mobile, from my waist south, nothing moved!

At this point the waiter, viewing my predicament smiled and said, "You've just been **Jacked!**" So that's where the word 'hi**jack**' comes from!

I said, "You've done this before haven't you?" To which he replied, "Yup, you're the **third** one I've 'Jacked' this week!"

Now over the years I've told this story on many occasions and every time I do it seems to polarise my audience. Half are disgusted that I could even possibly **contemplate** anything alcoholic at that time in the morning, while the opposing faction sidle up to me afterwards, to quietly enquire as to the **name** of the hotel in question!

As I've said before in this book, you can't get everyone's business, don't even try! There is a place in the market for those who prefer the ambience of the *Apple Blossom Inn* and also a place for those in the *'lush'* brigade who like a sparkle with the breakfast!

Just like the two funeral companies earlier, it is about deciding what your *brand* is and then communicating that to your designated *target audience*.

By *leading* with it in all your methods of communication you will *connect* with them more often; generating more sales, more profit.

# CHAPTER 11

# HOLD YOUR FIRE!

*Before spending on communications...*

In section 2.0, I urged a *ready, aim, fire* approach, in order to avoid missing target users with your message and wasting money in the process. If you've followed the book through to this point, your offering should be robust and nearly ready to launch to your target audience.

However this chapter covers some final checks to be considered before *the big bang!*

The first one is what to include in your description of your offering once people get past your *brand message* headline? In particular the need to balance the feeling of *simply having to introduce yourself*, with that of descriptive accuracy.

Also please make sure the copy you write makes sense. In this regard I would always try and get someone else to proof it first, not just for grammatical errors, but to ensure the message is coherent.

I remember receiving a promotional leaflet not long ago for home care products. Right on the front was a photograph of a can of air freshener at half price. It wasn't the monetary aspect of the leaflet that caught my eye, it was the wording which ran, "*Bring the scent of an Alpine spring meadow into your home. Freshen musty smelling rooms with exhilarating floral bouquets.*"

Then underneath was written in bold, **'WARNING: Inhaling contents can be harmful or fatal.'**

Somehow the two statements didn't quite gel, probably because one was written by *marketing* and the disclaimer by *legal*, each fighting their own corner. No one had stood back and tallied the two.

It is also important not to offer something that you will struggle to deliver. If claims can't be matched by the product or service then disappointment, mistrust and ultimately a bad reputation will follow.

Another area overlooked by many small enterprises is the grammar and wording used in their literature, advertisements, website and other forms of communications. In this regard much depends on *connecting* with your *target audience*. For example if they are in their teens or early twenties, there will be an entirely different style of writing and vocabulary, than that for the over sixties age group.

Whatever the style of writing and phraseology you use, please get it checked by someone who is part of that target group - it makes no sense at all asking someone your offering is not intended for to review your literature.

Proofing is essential and there are numerous stories of misspellings and other mistakes that have ruined marketing campaigns.

Shame-faced tourism chiefs from one area of Spain were forced to withdraw posters promoting the easy way of life in their region. Their concept was to run the campaign in UK travel magazines under the heading of *'Stand still'*, emphasising it was time to stop the world for a couple of weeks in the year.

Unfortunately a typo had occurred which absolutely nobody spotted. The letter 'd' in the word *'stand'* had been missed out, so it read instead, **'Stan** *still'*. What made this worse was that the model used in the accompanying photo was that of a young **lady!**

So instead of holiday enquiries they were instead inundated with requests from people wanting to know who 'Stan' was (and presumably how he managed to achieve such superbly hair-free shapely legs).

I have my own personal experience of such a thing, going way back in the mists of time. I once had to design and have printed a massive 60 foot banner for a high street menswear shop, promoting a *lost leader* sale line in their clearance event. The banner which was hung outside and ran the entire length of the shop front was to proudly declare, '**Men's polyester shirts only £1.99'.**

Unfortunately, as in the case of the Spanish tourist poster, I also accidentally missed out a letter. In my case however it was somewhat more indelicate, as the letter I omitted was the **'r'** in the word '*shirts*'

Unfortunately this was not spotted until the banner had been hung. I recall amused shoppers declaring they didn't know you could get such things in *polyester.*

To this day I always get someone else to check such communications, as the old '*can't* see the *wood for the trees*' expression is true. Often you can be too close to something and so need someone else to stand back and review it with fresh eyes.

## 11.1 Become your own customer...

### ...and see how you look!

Robert Burns, the national poet of Scotland once wrote, *'O' would some power the giftie gie us to see ourselves as others see us.'*

In business, being able to see your offering as other people view it, especially your *target audience*, is a **real** benefit. Putting yourself 100% in the position of the group you are aiming at and seeing your message through *their* eyes is however a difficult trick to pull off.

**Yet doing so is the *'secret'* to successful communication.**

Understanding the viewpoint of your prospective customers is key to connecting successfully with them. That is why I encourage all my clients, regardless of size, to engage with members of their target audience on a regular basis; even reward them for their time and input.

It is vital you know who your potential customers are, where are they, where do they visit, what values do they seek and what options do they have in terms of obtaining the product or service you can offer them?

Visit the websites or shops of your competitors to understand which direction they are moving in and what changes have they made since your last visit.

As your business begins to develop try and check how you are perceived by your customers; their likes and dislikes.

As we are living in an era of social media, begin dialoguing through these channels. That's not to say that you don't still need a website, but instead see that as more of a static *showroom*.

Facebook, Twitter and the myriad of other social media sites on the other hand, offer dialogue opportunities with actual and potential customers in **real time.**

This is the way to find out what is going on out there in your sector of the market, your golden opportunity to have a two way debate with the people who may well purchase your offering.

Become your own customer today and discover if you would do business with **you!**

## 11.2 The lost ramblers…

### …who walked off in the wrong direction!

In the last section we spoke about the importance of seeing your offering through the eyes of those you are targeting. Here is a good example of how by **not** doing this you can lose business by failing to *connect*.

I had just given an evening talk to a group of small business owners at a local hotel on the outskirts of Newcastle upon Tyne. I was trying to make my way to the bar (it's thirsty work marketing), when barring my path was a middle aged couple who had attended the lecture and plainly wanted to speak with me. Clearly my fantasies of a long cold pint of beer would have to be put on hold a little longer.

They explained that they had purchased a small hotel near the coast two years before. In that time they had revamped not only the accommodation itself but also their website, to try and attract more guests.

I asked them *'why you'* (well you **knew** I would!) and who their key *target audience* was. They explained that they were not a business hotel but primarily a **tourist** accommodation provider. Their key *why them* was that they were in an area of beautiful walks, one direction leading to the coastline and the other to pleasant countryside. Playing the role of a rambler, I then asked them how they would feel if I came into their newly decorated hotel dripping wet, wearing muddy boots? Their answer impressed me; they had converted a small utility room into an *overnight drying* area.

I went on to ask if there were any other facilities they had that proved how much they understood the pleasure of walking. Again their response was impressive. Packed lunches were available and the husband had drawn detailed maps of each route, including distances, approximate times and points of interest along the way. They even offered to come in their car and collect guests who had walked too far! All in all I was impressed and promised to have a look at their website the next day; in the meantime I had another appointment to keep... at the bar!

The next day I duly visited their website which although attractively laid out, completely omitted to make any mention of the benefits which the owners had told me about the night before. There was nothing about the drying room, maps, or packed lunches just a sentence on the walks nearby.

By visiting their website with my *rambler's* hat on these were facilities I was **looking for.** As someone who was seeking *walker-friendly* accommodation, if good facilities were not evident I would probably go elsewhere - **failed connection, lost business.**

So please put yourself 100% in position of your target customers and see things through their eyes - that's what I would do if you were my client. I'd establish who you were aiming at, become that person and then examine your offering.

## 11.3 The most important day of your life...
### ...would *you* say 'I do?'

This next example is similar to the *Ramblers* except it has an additional dimension that I think worth covering.

Again it concerns a hotel that I was invited to visit; consisting of 20 bedrooms, spacious gardens, bar, restaurant and function room. It is around the last of these facilities, the *function room* that the story centres.

The hotel owner explained that while they enjoyed satisfactory levels of occupancy on the accommodation side of the business, there was considerable capacity for more bookings on functions.

When I looked at their website, the reason became all too obvious. The buttons on the Home page read as follows:

**About us** | **Rooms** | **Restaurant** | **Functions** | **Area** | **Contact**

While on the face of it this may seem a reasonable menu, please put yourself in the position of let's say a couple planning their big day and looking for somewhere for a reception venue.

First of all there was nothing on the Home page to *connect* with them, no mention of the word '*Wedding*'. When I clicked the *Functions* tab there was a general description of the size of the room, a photograph showing it when empty and then a paragraph saying that it was suitable for parties, anniversaries, Christmas and *they could also do Weddings*.

*"**Do** Weddings?"*

And the hotel owner wondered why there weren't more bookings for weddings?! Imagine the position of the prospective happy couple. This is supposed (I am reliably informed) to be the happiest day of your life; so would you really want to spend this in a hotel that could **do** a wedding?!

Instead the website should have a **dedicated** 'Weddings' button on the Home page that immediately connects to that particular target audience. Push that button and you enter into 'your day' and everything the venue has to offer to make it a perfect one.

Of course it isn't only wedding parties who wish to book a function room, how about **business?** There are many companies who plan away days for their management team, or even larger business conferences. Yet the same situation applies as with the weddings; there is no mention of this on the Home page of the site, nothing to connect with this target audience.

Instead of giving each one of these real target audiences a **dedicated** button of their own, the hotel had instead 'fudged' them all together under the 'functions' button - **not good!** If each had their own button it would immediately connect them with their respective target group, which in turn would lead to more time being spent examining the offering and a greater likelihood of a positive outcome.

If a similar situation applies to **your** enterprise i.e. you have more than one target audience for your offering, then please don't bundle them up together, but instead allow each one the freedom to connect with its own target audience and express itself.

Remember this applies not only to your website but sales literature as well.

## 11.4 Call to 'action'...

### ...direct your audience!

When compiling content for your communications, be it advertising, literature or website; remember to include one very important element, **'a call to action!'**

One of the biggest mistakes businesses of all sizes make is not having this and it never fails to amaze me that a company can take time and spend money telling prospective customers about their offering and then **leave it at that!**

Instead, at every stage regardless of what form of communication you are using, tell potential customers what you'd like them to do next. I'm not necessarily saying you instruct them to **buy,** although even that is better than nothing, but just guide them to the next stage.

So for example if you are advertising a new product of service, after giving the benefits provide the reader with a link for *further information,* or invite them to request a *'free information pack',* or *'apply today for a quotation',* or go on a *'mailing list for future updates',* or even just, *'visit our website for full details'.*

Deadlines too are important to stress; so if an offer is **time-limited** emphasise this to inject some urgency into their actions. For example if holding a sale then please add how long the event is going to last - *'Hurry, finishes this Saturday'*, or *'One day only!'*, or *'January Sale, 7-14th'*.

If it is **stock** of a line that is limited (*'while stocks last'*) then this is very important to mention and on your website you may even quote the number left, adjusting this as sales come in. Again this instils a degree of urgency into the deliberations of the target audience; the old marketing adage, *'when they're gone, they're gone!'*

On this theme, I once produced marketing for a country rock band with the goal of getting them a recording contract in *America*.

We were successful in getting a video of their single on the playlist of CMTV (Country Music Television). I then checked that week's current station playlist and discovered that every artist, except the act I was marketing had been *'signed'* by a record label. There were some of the very biggest names on the list including, *Shania Twain, Sting, Eric Clapton* and *Dolly Parton*.

I wrote to every major record label enclosing a copy of the band's DVD, something of course they receive every day of the week. However I added a **'call to action'** by saying, "There are *58 artists on the current CMT playlist - **57** are 'signed'*, **one** *isn't.... **but for how long?**"

In this way people in the music industry were motivated to act, through fear of losing out on a potential future star.

In a similar way if you have a special offer, that is limited in quantity, tell people this! *'Offer limited to the first 50 enquirers.'* If however you have a new line altogether then add phrases like, *'call for a preview'*, or *'come and see what the future looks like'*, or *'register now for further details'*.

Work out the best pathway for directing customers to your offering and evaluate enquiry responses at each stage, so you know what has worked and when.

## 11.5 Communication = cost...
### ...so try sharing it

Many years ago I remember watching a television commercial that had something in it I hadn't seen before. It was for *Hotpoint* washing machines; however it was *also* for another product manufactured by a different company. Although on the face of it this may seem a little strange it is really very clever marketing.

The other product was *Persil*, a washing powder and the commercial carried the message, *'Hotpoint recommends Persil'*.

For me this form of *strategic alliance* works on a number of levels. Firstly the two products have a synergy, they are connected in the process of cleaning clothes, one is the machine in which they are washed and the other is the detergent that removes (with the help of the machine's movement) dirt and stains.

*In short, they are both targeting **the same end-user,** but are **not in competition** with each other.*

What's more this type of alliance can offer other benefits, including **cost sharing.** For example if two products can strike up an alliance similar to *Hotpoint* and *Persil* then they may be able to share the costs of promotion, as both are receiving exposure.

If two companies come together in this way and decide to go 50/50 in terms of sharing advertising, they can either receive the same exposure for 50% less cost, or **double** their amount of exposure for the **same** cost they would otherwise have faced if going it alone.

There is yet another potential benefit to this type of *buddying-up.* By each recommending the other, they can enjoy the reflected glory of the other's endorsement. Of course partners must be picked carefully!

Why I am mentioning all this in a book aimed at *start-up* and *small businesses* is that I continually try to get my clients to consider if there are any strategic alliances they can form and I'd like to issue the same challenge to **you** now.

Remember the golden rule is that you and your alliance partner should be aiming for the same end user, but **not** be in **competition** with each other. An example of one such alliance I instigated was when I had two clients, one a florist who among other occasions specialised in *wedding flowers,* including buttonholes and table decorations. The other was a company that sold and hired *bridal wear.*

While both were clearly targeting the same client, they were not in competition with each other. This meant they could work together in areas such as window displays, where each would include a display card on the other's company. Likewise on their websites they exchanged a link to the other's site and also included photography that featured both products; a bride in wedding dress holding a bridal bouquet.

None of these cost any money but helped increase exposure to the right *target audience* in a way they previously had not had access to.

They also shared stand space at exhibitions, reducing costs and attracting the possibility of dual sales from the one customer. The last time I spoke with them they were considering extending their circle of *alliance partners* to include a local cake shop that specialises in wedding cakes.

So bearing in mind this example, is there a company that **you** know that is aiming at the same target group as your own offering, but yet is not in direct competition with you? If there is please consider getting together with them, increasing your exposure **and** reducing those promotional costs.

## 11.6 Involve your staff...

### ...or they can be 'terminal' for business

I hope that if this book achieves nothing else, it will at least have conveyed the importance of establishing clearly what your *brand* is. It is the bedrock of your business and your *brand promise* will be the rallying call that leads you into battle.

However all this can be undone, not by your competitors, but inadvertently by your own side... **your staff!** Failure to bring them with you in terms of **grasping** your *brand* can lead to failure.

I remember once driving a long distance to arrive at an independent hotel called the *Friendly Place*. After the tedious journey I just wanted to have a shower and a drink, but not necessarily in **that** order! I made my way to check-in where the receptionist was on the phone, so I waited… and waited… and waited.

During this time which stretched well over 10 minutes, she made no attempt to acknowledge my presence even though she had seen me arrive, nor did she give me any signal to indicate how long she would be. Eventually, fed up of being ignored, I asked her if anyone else could perhaps check me in. With a 5 star withering look, she covered the mouthpiece of the phone and said, "I'm on the phone!"

Talk about stating the bl\*\*dy obvious! I decided however against confirming that my powers of observation had indeed recorded this fact and instead ventured, "Sorry, but can anyone else check me in then as I've been waiting nearly 15 minutes?" Hesitating for a moment she then said to the person on the other end of the phone, "Karen I'm going to have to call you back!"

Then without a hint of apology, or even as much as a glance in my direction she said, *"Name?"*

This was my introduction, as a **customer,** to the **Friendly Place.** The entire *brand* of the hotel had been totally wrecked by one member of staff who was annoyed at my flagrant audacity in interrupting her **personal** conversation. Thank god for the likes of *Trip Advisor* nowadays!

Another example and an altogether more humorous one was when I was invited to meet with the owner of a car accessories mini-supermarket. On my arrival I was impressed to see that above the door was a sign announcing proudly his *brand promise*, *'Your local expert in car accessories'*.

*"Good for him"*, I thought.

I entered and approached the checkout where a young girl was pricing stock; I told her I had an appointment with the owner. She disappeared to get him, returning a few moments later to inform me that he was just finishing another meeting and would be with me shortly.

While waiting I walked round the store assessing how in-depth his range of accessories was. While doing this a guy came in, looking a little flushed, had a quick look round and not seeing what he was looking for headed for the assistant, "Do you have any jump-leads?"

The young girl thought for a moment, as if trying to recall their whereabouts and then set off down one of the aisles. What happened next was pure comedy gold. With a note of triumph in her voice she shouted, "Yes we have them; do you want **red** or **black**?!"

Bearing in mind the shop's *brand promise* of, *'Your local* **expert** *in car accessories'*, you can see what can happen when members of staff aren't properly trained in either product or *brand*.

If **you** are looking to grow a good reputation in **your** business, please bring your staff with you and invest time in them. Getting them to share your vision really can **jump-start** your business.

# CHAPTER 12

# YOUR BEST SALES PEOPLE? YOUR CUSTOMERS!

### Consult them, love them…
### 'employ' them

I want to look briefly ahead in this section to what happens when your *brand* is a success, sales start to flow and you find yourself with that most valuable of commodities… **customers!**

So what do you do with them? My advice would be to try and complete as much of the following list as possible:

✓ **File them** - Compiling a database is much easier if your business is an online one, as ready-made software will help you log all details. Even when the sale is made in a shop, still try and collect as much information as possible on your customer. You can do this by having a small card printed, asking for their email address to keep them updated. Give them this at point of sale, or drop it into the bag with their goods.

✓ **Email them** - Please remember to ask specifically for their permission if emailing them and on each email give them the opportunity to withdraw from this scheme.

✓ **Love them** - If you have been successful in obtaining their email address, use it (sparingly) to notify them **first** of special offers, new ranges, or sale events, **before** the general public are informed. People love to feel they have won a special privilege and usually reward those who have bestowed it on them.

✓ **Consult them** - Most businesses *move on* in terms of ranges stocked or new services introduced. Prior to implementing either of these why not reduce the risk of them not being popular by asking for the opinion of your customers. People like to be involved and have their opinion taken into account, providing it is for something that they have an interest in.

✓ **Employ them** - I don't mean to put them on the payroll, but to encourage testimonials from them, or reward them if they 'recruit' new customers from their circle of contacts. If you do offer an incentive I'd strongly recommend that it applies to **both** the new as well as the existing customer. That way they both feel a benefit and both are more likely to go on recommending.

By friends introducing each other in this way you are spared much of the normal sales process **and** your promotions budget is spent only when business is actually received!

Remember **word of mouth** always has and always will be the best form of advertising. That's why turning customers into **ambassadors** for your company's offering really can work.

*You may find they will be your most **loyal and productive sales force**.*

## 12.1 The last testament...
*...the most powerful advertising -
customer recommendations!*

Picking up where we left off in the last section I want to focus a little more on *customer feedback and testimonials*. Today we live in such a *social media* society that we readily share our experiences with others, some we know and many we don't.

This is certainly true when it comes to our experiences of holidays, hotels, restaurants, purchases made across the whole retail sector, especially online buys.

*...the most powerful advertising -*
*customer recommendations!*

What's more, as consumers we rely and even trust on these comments made by others who were once in the same position as us. Even though we don't know the people we believe they are genuine and impartial, they are telling us the way they found things for **our** benefit.

Conversely although we'd often **like** to believe the marketing hype surrounding products and services we're interested in, as portrayed by those selling them, we are more cautious, even suspicious.

More and more websites that have retail facilities offer customer feedback for site visitors to read. Some of these customer reports are very involved, but helpful, others are short and to the point.

I'm grateful to the friend of mine who sent me the following customer feedback he had seen on an *Adult Toys* website, which he'd accidentally landed on while searching for an electric toothbrush, it ran…

**Item purchased:** *Vib. XL2*

**Customer feedback:** *Neat bit of kit - only has two speed settings, but both are powerful enough to mess with the signal on my television. It actually changed channels twice while I was fiddling with it.*

It's hard to work out whether **that** customer product feedback is a positive or a negative, but as my TV remote is currently on the blink it could be a **real** plus.

That to one side, how can **you** encourage and then **use** testimonials? First of all if you are selling online direct from your own site, once the goods are delivered or the service installed, simply ask for feedback. Perhaps this could be as an online form headed: *'How did we do?'*

If you are any kind of tradesperson who works on people's property, then on completion **always** ask the customer to enter their comments on the form they use to sign the job off.

If you are an accommodation provider do the same; ask guests to make an entry in your guest book, then place their words on your website, under '*What our guests say*'. Here's the critical part - **always enter the date!**

If you can, add these weekly, even daily if possible. There is nothing more persuasive for potential clients than to see positive comments from a satisfied customer that are just a day or two old. It means that your offering has been judged to be good **now!**

Many businesses are making room on the Home page of their websites for customer comments, making a feature out of them. If you do not want to use the full name of the person who has supplied the comments then perhaps just use their initials.

Glowing testimonials have the effect of making companies work harder to get even better comments, as they know that these will have a positive impact on driving future business.

I also will list comments I receive from people such as **you** who have invested the cover price of this book. So if you feel I have repaid your faith and given good value for money and made a genuine attempt to help you please go online and say so!

Finally, always enter the most **recent** *customer comment* at the top of the list, as the **last testament** is always the most powerful, in the eyes of those reading them.

# CHAPTER 13

# PUTTING IT ALL TOGETHER

*- a glass act!*

theglazingguy.com

Rather than merely list a summary of the key points in *Stand-up Marketing*, I thought it might be a better idea to bring them to life through examples in this chapter.

So in 13.1 and 13.2 we look at two start-up businesses, beginning to make their way in the market and consider the key elements they have included to strengthen their offering and help *make the connection* with their *target audience*.

But first let's *build a business* using a hypothetical example. Let's assume that someone who has trained as a *glazier* wants to start his own small enterprise. First as we know, he has to work out his place in his chosen market. He begins with *Home Improvements* as his overall marketplace and then segments down to the *Glazing* sector.

This is still way too big for him to try and compete and so he further segments until he arrives at a sub-sector called *replacement glazing,* a niche where he believes his offering works best and he can build from.

His *replacement glazing* service will encompass emergencies and windows that have become damaged and misted through time. He will target both *domestic* and *commercial* users. By finding his corner of the market in this way he will avoid the *big beasts* in the jungle and begin to grow business roots.

Next he needs a trading name! As we spoke about earlier in the book it is better for credibility's sake that he doesn't try and look bigger than he actually is, in fact he **wants** to **celebrate** his size because he can then offer a quicker, more personalised service.

He also wants a name that he can match with a website address, so he has the two in one. Before deciding on his trading name he therefore tries to find one with an available domain name. He finally goes for **The Glazing Guy,** with a website address of, www.theglazingguy.com (for the purposes of this book I have secured this domain, so no need to check it out!).

As a trading name, *The Glazing Guy* rejoices in his small size and introduces a personal note that he very much wants to become his *brand.* He desires to offer the kind of service that **he** would like to receive from someone coming into **his** home.

His *brand* and *why me* features will therefore include:

✓ Turning up punctually and if for any reason running late, calling ahead to advise the customer.

✓ Wearing a uniform of branded sweatshirt and blue trousers. The front of the sweatshirt has his name and logo, the back is emblazoned with his *brand promise,* **'A glass act'.**

✓ When arriving at the customer's property, presenting his security ID badge, complete with photograph.

✓ If a wet day, wearing shoe covers when entering the property.

✓ Laying down dust covers both inside and out, to catch glass or debris from the old window and frame.

✓ Once the new window has been installed, cleaning it on both the inside and out.

- ✓ Vacuuming inside the property (with his own vacuum cleaner he keeps in the van).

- ✓ Removing the old window from the customer's property as well as any debris.

- ✓ Leaving the customer a bottle of *window cleaner,* with his compliments.

- ✓ Leaving them with a fridge magnet with his telephone number on *in case of emergencies*

- ✓ The customer is also given a *'recommend a friend'* leaflet and should they purchase at any time from him, *both* the new and existing customer will receive a £5.00 *Marks and Spencer* food voucher.

Once the installation is complete he asks the customer to sign a satisfaction form **and** invites them to enter any comments they may have in a box at the bottom. If he has lived up to his *brand promise* of, A *Glass Act* he will be rewarded with a glowing testimonial.

Later that day he enters the customer's remarks together with the initials of their name on his website under, *'Customer comments'*. He also enters the date and places the most recent entry at the top of the list.

Because he has two distinct *target audiences, domestic* and *commercial,* he has two sections on his website so customers from each can immediately identify the section that is suited to their requirements.

His *branding* shows the **.com** added to his name, so it is easy to identify his website. His van is decaled with both his *identity* and in large letters his *brand promise.*

One week later he gives a quick courtesy call to his customer to make sure everything is still to their satisfaction. While there he drops cards through the doors of houses in the vicinity, mentioning he has just completed a job for one of their neighbours and inviting them to go online to see what they thought of his work.

In this way *The Glazing Guy* will begin to develop a strong *brand* of *excellence in customer care*, this will increasingly lead to an equally positive *reputation* which in turn will generate more business through his network of customer ambassadors.

Truly, *a glass act.*

## 13.1 Picturing the right environment...
### ...the OTHER Tate Gallery!

In this chapter, *Putting it all together* I wanted to finish with two examples of small businesses who in very different fields are beginning to breakthrough and emerge as established businesses.

Like many in this book, both of these examples have allowed their enterprise to be included, in the hope it will help other small business owners - which is pretty damn amazing!

I have chosen this first case as it is a great example of a small business *positioning* itself in a niche market, clearly *identifying* those who would benefit from its service and then *making a connection* with the designated *target audience*.

I first met *Jill Tate* in a *mentoring session* at *Northumbria University* and was immediately struck by her focus of direction for her craft. Her intention was clear, to develop this craft into a *business*.

Jill is a photographer and a very talented one at that. Although the overall *Photography* market is a massive one she has segmented down to a particular niche that she describes as, '*architecture and the built environment*'.

This means that as a freelance photographer she *specialises* in architecture, construction, interiors and landscapes, providing high quality, unique images for a range of clients.

Jill can explain better than I, why she chose this sector of the market to establish her business, "I photograph architecture and interior spaces to communicate my fascination with the built environment. I have always been captivated by light, colour and geometry, and find that buildings offer endless possibility to explore this."

As Jill had already selected her niche in the market we began by considering who her *target audience* for such an offering would be. We concluded that the architecture, design and construction industries could all benefit from the striking imagery she produces, helping them convey the quality of their work for archival and promotional purposes.

Next we had to find an appropriate way of making the *connection* between her offering and this target group. As Jill was at that time only just starting out and with a limited budget we had to be creative in our approach.

I immediately identified one major plus factor Jill had at her disposal... her name, *Tate*. We decided to showcase her work in the following way. On her website Jill opened a gallery of photographs for each season of the year. We called each collection her, *Spring Exhibition, Summer Exhibition* and so on.

From these we selected one image and produced it as a landscape postcard, bleeding the image off the sides to make it more striking. We then added the following title to the front of the cards, '*The (**other**) Tate Gallery*'.

As we had these digitally printed, we were able to keep the print run down to the 80 she required to reach her main *target audience*.

The striking images on the front of the cards stood out from other items of post, when delivered to design, architecture and construction companies. We repeated the exercise each quarter announcing that season's exhibition, monitoring the results as we went.

The first indication that Jill was indeed *making a connection* was in the increase of visitor numbers to her online exhibitions. These visits correlated to the dates of the cards being mailed and so we knew people were beginning to take note of her offering.

Then as the seasons progressed the number of enquiries grew and Jill began receiving more commissions. Combining a fresh approach and a keen eye for detail she consistently delivers dynamic, eye-catching images for her clients and their feedback has been extremely positive.

As such Jill is now becoming an established enterprise with repeat business and her services increasingly in demand.

**www.jilltate.com**

## 13.2 It's in the bag...

*... a sunny outlook for a rainwear company*

I never cease to be amazed at the ingenuity of product designers; their brains are clearly wired entirely differently to my own. When I see a clever design I immediately *get it* and understand the benefits, although I could never have conceived of the idea myself. My DNA is devoid of the design gene.

This is not the case in this next small business example, where a mother has clearly passed on her designing ability to her daughter and between them they are making quite a *splash* in the rainwear business.

Their product **Baggers** is creatively brilliant! It is a range of rainwear for children that when not needed quite literally tucks back into its own pocket to form a bag for them to carry. It is the perfect way to conveniently store rainwear until the weather turns bad and then carry wet outerwear home after the rain stops.

While Angela, the mother, developed the concept many years ago, it is her daughter Jessica and a small youthful team who are **now** helping her drive it forward.

To ensure that their *brand* concept is right for today's market, they conducted detailed research with their key *target audience* and included likely *retail prices* as part of this investigation (which as discussed earlier in this book is so important when conducting research).

Following on from this research the company is very clear about *direction* and their *'why us'* benefits. The children love them for the bold colours, plus the *'magic'* fold-away feature; whereas their parents welcome the fact that their kids can go out without having to take additional clothing in case it rains. With *Baggers* if a shower should arrive, their child will be protected against the wet in a matter of seconds.

The team are now about to launch a new *swimwear* range, again with the same clever fold-away feature for storage and carrying.

At the time of writing this book the company have been selected to appear in a BBC television programme on small business that will do much to highlight their offering to a nationwide audience. They are also in discussions with a well-known UK retail chain regarding stocking the product.

Working on the branding with the *Baggers* team was a fun experience for me, but I have to credit *them* for the company's *brand promise*, which I think is also a description of their likely success in the future... **'It's in the bag!'**

**www.baggersoriginals.com**

## CHAPTER 14

# SPEAK WITH ME ONLINE, ONE-TO-ONE

*Potentially the most important business conversation you will ever have*

In one of *Sherlock Holmes* stories, 'A *Study in Scarlet'*, *Holmes* explains to *Watson* that he need not necessarily attend a crime scene in order to solve it. He argues that if the facts are laid before him and he has done it one thousand times before, why shouldn't he therefore be able to solve it on the thousandth and first?

In many ways my online *one-to-one* service is exactly like that, except that I have *'done it'* much more than just one thousand times! I don't need to be at the actual business premises to help the business owner. As long as I am well briefed on the background to the company's situation I am as likely to be able to help online as if I were physically there.

However there is one major difference - **cost!** Meeting online via *Skype* or similar greatly reduces the cost of my consultation time, by around 75% compared to seeing me in the flesh (probably nicer too!).

I have to charge for this service, because like you I am a small business that needs to generate an income to survive. However the return on your investment can pay healthy dividends - so I believe it is an investment really worth making.

The charges are listed on my website and as you have already purchased my book there is an introductory offer of 25% discount on your first consultation, which will recover the price you paid for this book! To claim this you simply have to enter the following code word on my website: 'MARKETING'.

This service also means that we can 'meet' wherever you are in the world! Last year I undertook similar one-to-one sessions with people in the UK,

Canada, Tenerife, France, Switzerland, America, Germany and Saudi Arabia. If we are creative in our time management, differences in time zones can be overcome.

So what does this service cover? Well in general terms it can involve; coaching, mentoring, strategy, campaigns, promotions, brand, branding, *why you* and competition. In more detailed terms it can include any topic contained in this book.

It is really about letting my experiences shine some light into your business. This can apply if it is going well and you are considering moving up to the next level. It can also help you overcome challenges you are currently facing.

It could be that you haven't got as many customers as you need, or that you are getting enquiries but failing to convert these numbers into sales. Your *brand* perception may be weak, or perhaps you are struggling to be seen in a crowded market, or maybe would like to devise an attention-grabbing campaign.

It may be that you have not yet gone into business and just want to discuss your plans and get feedback.

If you believe that things are beginning to go wrong I urge you to **act fast** - don't lie down, **stand-up** and let's try and get things back on track.

Whatever we discuss, please know this. I will bring to bear every ounce of experience I possess to assist you. *Everything we discuss will be in complete confidence.*

There are two options regarding length of consultation, either a thirty minute or one hour sitting. The longer one hour session works out to be more cost effective and allows time to develop themes, but the choice is yours. Follow-up sessions, or regular mentoring will also attract a discount.

You will be amazed at just how much ground we can cover in an hour and what can be achieved. You may also be surprised at just how many ideas I will fire at you for your consideration.

Whatever your business, whatever its size, this is a unique opportunity to speak with me one-to-one and who knows it could just be the most important conversation in your company's history.

**Full details of the service are on my website:**
**www.standupmarketing.com**

---

### 25% discount offer!

As someone who has purchased this book you are entitled to 25% discount off your first one-to-one online consultation with John.

Go to www.standupmarketing.com for full details and enter code: MARKETING

Offer lasts until December 31st 2013.

---

# CHAPTER 15
# AU REVOIR...

*...until the next time we meet*

Well if you have stayed with me this far I'd like to thank you; a great deal of work and planning has gone into this book and it really makes it worth while to know that someone has actually **read** it!

Of course it will be all the **more** worthwhile if you actually **benefit** from some of the advice or examples contained in it. If you do please email and let me know!

People who are not in business can never truly understand what we small enterprise owners go through; an emotional rollercoaster of soaring highs and occasionally, desperate lows.

By coming out from behind the parapet, trusting in **your** belief and committing **your** endeavour, you are doing something truly amazing by going into business. You have the respect and support of me and I'm sure all others who have trodden the same path.

As a small business owner you are part of an exclusive club, whose membership is as enterprising as it is hard-working, as innovative as it is crazy and as determined as it is courageous.

The aims of this book were firstly, to get the 'ready' and 'aim' parts of the 'ready, aim, fire,' formula clear in your mind, so when you do begin to spend money on communicating, you are much more likely to hit the target. The second aim was to make you **smile** in parts and I hope in some measure I may have achieved both.

In case you are wondering if a sequel to this book is planned, the answer is, yes! I'd really like to complete the formula and help you with the 'fire' part, guiding you through the myriad of ways there are for a small business to communicate your *brand* and your *why you* benefits to the *target audience.*

So please watch my website for details and add your name to my mailing list, so I can keep you updated. In the meantime I will close by wishing you everything that is good in business and hope that one day we will meet in person.

Until then I'll leave you with one final thought; if anything that I have said in this book helps you go on to become truly successful and fabulously wealthy, then please know this…

*I'm open to* **retrospective payments!**

# CHAPTER 16
# CURTAIN CALL

*Thanks to those without whose help this book wouldn't have been possible (so blame THEM if you didn't like it!)*

I'd like to express my thanks to those people who have both directly and indirectly contributed to this book. This is also my opportunity to give thanks to those who due to the daily dash through life never quite receive the acknowledgement from me that they deserve.

## Artistic contributors to this book

Regarding the actual production of this book I would like to recognise the following people and companies. Having been in marketing for many years and therefore well connected to suppliers, printers, photographers and designers, I decided to keep the ethos of this book by working instead with young, small businesses.

In particular I wanted to involve people who although maybe experienced and talented had never quite done this type of project before; to use their creative energies and see what the outcome would be!

## PRINT AND DESIGN

I *must* begin by giving a huge *thank-you* to **Rob Gibbons** of *your Print Department,* for an amazing effort in the design and printing of this book. Although greatly experienced in all forms of digital, litho and wide format printing, Rob wanted to produce for the first time a book from scratch and what you are holding now is the *result!*

Although based in the northeast of England, his company provide design and printing services for organisations across the country, delivering to all corners of the UK. They are a small business's best friend, offering themselves as an additional resource, an extra department; *your Print Department!*

Rob also facilitated my working with his designer **Jo Spottiswood** on both *branding* and *layout* for the book. Jo, your stress ball must be worn thin, but you never once complained; *'You kept calm and carried on!'* Many thanks for a quite superb design job.

From planning advice, through to design and on to final print, the collaboration with *your Print Department's* team of Rob, Sally, Nicola and Jo has been 5-star. I'd recommend them unreservedly to any business.

**www.yourprintdepartment.co.uk**

## DESIGN INPUT

### Tom Purvis

Tom, I have worked with you on more design projects than there are words in this book! You have produced some fantastic outcomes, working long into the night on many occasions to meet a deadline. Thanks for your support and loyalty over the years; you are one of life's true gentlemen.

Design input - sections: 3.1, 4.1, 4.2, 5.0, 6.2, 6.4, 6.5, 7.2, 8.4, 9.2, 9.3, 10.0, 10.1, 10.3, 13.0, 13.1

## PHOTOGRAPHY

### Anthony Dorman Photography

In my career I have worked with many gifted photographers, but staying with my brief of trying where possible to work with young companies for the book, I chose Anthony Dorman and a damn good choice it proved!

Anthony takes time to ensure he has full grasp of the brief and then works **fast!** I was exhausted by the end of our shoot, but had a smile on my face as wide as the River Tyne, as I knew how well it had gone.

Anthony has not just an eye for a photograph, but a sixth sense for one; he feels it, captures it, all in an instant. Here is a little about his background:

*'I picked up a camera to document a trip to Thailand a few years back and what started as holiday snaps turned into a true passion for photography. Having spent 10 torturous years in retail I finally had the chance in January 2011 to turn my passion into a business. Although I will mainly be found wandering the streets of Newcastle taking portraits of random strangers I also work on a mixture of portrait, product and commercial work for individuals and companies alike. Photography has truly opened my eyes to the world and has introduced me to fantastic people and places I would never have seen otherwise.'*

**www.anthonydormanphotography.blogspot.co.uk**

Anthony Dorman Photography - sections: 1.3, 2.0, 3.1, 4.0, 4.2, 5.0, 5.3, 6.0, 7.0, 7.1, 8.0, 8.2, 9.0, 9.1, 9.2 (Dixie), 10.0, 10.5, 11.1, 11.2, 11.4, 11.6, 12.0, 14.0

Thanks also to Mayfield Photographic Studio, Newcastle upon Tyne.

## Gavin Duthie, photography

Gavin Duthie is one of northeast England's best photographers. He is equally at home shooting landscape vistas, as industrial surroundings and documentary shots of people.

Gavin, you and I have worked together on many projects over the years and the consistent high quality of the work you produce is quite amazing. Many thanks for your contribution to the sections of this book as listed below.

Photography - sections: 5.1, 10.4, 11.0,

www.gavinduthie.com

## Stock photography

Photos - sections: 1.0, 1.1, 1.2, 3.0, 4.1, 5.0, 5.2, 6.1, 6.2, 6.3, 6.4, 6.5, 7.0, 7.1, 8.0, 8.1, 8.3, 9.2, 10.0, 10.3, 11.3, 11.5, front cover, back cover

www.istockphoto.com

www.shutterstock.com

## MODELS

### Laura Jane Carson

You're a fantastic model Laura, to dress (or **undress**) to play the role of Dixie so superbly at 9.00AM on a Saturday morning was quite brilliant! Many thanks too for the great collar-up shots.

Photographs - sections: 5.0, 9.2

### Matt Kay

Matt thanks for being the 'tall' to my 'short'! You were great to work with and very best wishes for your own business career.

Photograph - section: 5.3

## PROOFING

### Dawn Stroz

When looking for someone to proof this book I wanted somebody to understand its heart and direction and make sure it **didn't** read like a text book.

Dawn, you achieved this, proofing at all times and places, such as taxis, trains, boats and planes, from the frozen tundra of Canada, to the **really** frozen climate of Aberdeen!

I know in the past you have proofed **political** publications - so what was it like working on a book that wasn't **fiction?!** Amazing job, this is what you do… *if proof were needed.*

## WEBSITE

### Adam Brewer, Peacockish

Thanks to my very talented website designer and budding entrepreneur in his own right, who is developing some great online businesses.

Adam, despite the near impossible parking at your place, followed by the **great ascent** of six flights of stairs to get to your office - when I do get my breath back it's always fun working with you. Top website, thanks mate.

**www.peacockish.com**

## SEARCH ENGINE OPTIMISATION (SEO)

### Matt Waterman

Thanks M, for your true friendship over the years and for helping me achieve page one status in the search engines - **no one** does it better than you!

**www.mattseo.com**

## BUSINESSES FEATURED IN THIS BOOK

My sincere thanks go to the following individuals and companies for agreeing to share some of their own story in this book. Each has generously done this in the hope that their experiences will help new businesses get a foothold and begin to grow.

This is a wonderful example of networking that I'm sure will be appreciated by those who read the book, (who in time when successful will hopefully do likewise for other new businesses). *We're in this together.*

Business name in alphabetical order:

**Acorn Van Hire** (Mark Ryder)
Many thanks Mark, you are my nomination for *entrepreneur of the year!*
www.acornvanhire.co.uk

**Assembly and Packaging Services** (Judith Leighton)
Judith thank you for allowing me to feature *APS* in the book; the project we worked on together more than a few years ago now is still one of the best I've ever been involved with. I'm so pleased that your hard work and real commitment to providing a superior service is continuing to be recognised by major organisations.
www.assemblyandpackagingservices.co.uk

**Atul and Chitra Malkar, Kartik Poojari**
To three of the nicest people I have met; you have been through a lot, but always stay committed. When success comes it will be well deserved.

**Baggers Originals** (Angela and Jessica McLean)

Angie and Jessica, you are two of my best friends in business and I am so pleased for you both that such great design innovation as your *Baggers* product, is finding a new audience, a new generation.

www.baggersoriginals.com

**Big River Films** (Alastair Cummings and Richard Power)

Alastair and Richard; well despite you two NEVER having any bloody coffee, it's been fantastic working with you. Whether it's been fighting 'sharks' in the sea, power-boating up the Tyne, or filming commercials for wigs, it's been brilliant! You *are* filmmakers.

www.bigriverfilms.co.uk

**Berwick Garden Centre** (Nick Crabbie)

Nick, I'm pleased to have spoken to you again recently and learned of your expansion plans. I very much enjoyed working together with you several years ago and to see it has worked so well. Thanks for permitting me to include you in this book.

www.berwick-gardencentre.co.uk

**Fast Forward Now** (Angela McLean)

Angie, you have done so much to help enterprise students, community entrepreneurs and other small businesses become established. I am therefore glad you have been recognised, winning some significant awards. Thank you also for supporting my *Stand-up marketing* lectures.

www.fastforwardnow.com

**Fresh and Filling** (Mark Ryder)

Mark, this is another bit of *'fresh'* thinking by you - where **do** you get your inspiration… **and** energy! Have enjoyed working with you over many years and look forward to many more.

**Garbeau** (Jessica McLean)

Jessica, you have in my opinion transformed a stuffy market into one that is fresh and dynamic. I love the little, but so important touches, that you have brought to the market. You are a great fashion designer and it's been lovely working with you!

www.garbeau.eu

**Hazelrigg Bed and Breakfast** (Lorna Harrison)

Thanks Lorna for sharing your story! I'm so pleased that your very own marketing talents, combined with the hard work and dedication you have put in, are giving you the success you richly deserve.

www.hazelriggbandb.com

**Howick Hall Gardens** (Lord Howick)

My thanks go to Lord Howick for his kind permission to include the advertisement for the very beautiful Howick Hall Gardens and Arboretum.

www.howickhallgardens.org

**Jill Tate Photography** (Jill Tate)

Thanks for allowing inclusion of your story Jill; I'm really pleased your talent and dedication are being widely recognised and commissioned.

www.jilltate.com

**Milk to Perfection** (Graeme Stewart)

Graeme, I really enjoyed working with you on the *Milk to Perfection* project. You are a true original thinker with the determination to match and I look forward to watching your progress in the future!

www.milktoperfection.co.uk

**Northumbria Healthcare NHS Foundation Trust**

I have enjoyed a long association with Northumbria Healthcare, an organisation that I have a great deal of affection and respect for. I could have filled this book with examples of innovative work they are doing to help improve journeys and outcomes for patients. I am pleased to have been able to include one example of how they also care for their staff, through the *Health and Wellbeing* programme.

www.northumbria.nhs.uk

**Paul Reynolds** (Renown Estates)

Really good speaking with you again recently Paul; seems a very long time since we worked together on your project and yet it is still clear in my memory. For me your specialist knowledge was and still is your key strength. It is much appreciated that you shared part of your story.

www.renownestates.com

**Ski-Reg** (Reg Pound)

Reg, everyone I know who has spent time in your company goes away with a smile on their face; you are *that* type of special person! It is great to have been able to feature you in this book and I look forward to seeing you and Mary again soon on the *Island of Eternal Spring.* In the meantime Reg, *'keep getting them up!'*

www.skireg.co.uk

**Weigh-ahead UKENA Ltd** (Gerard, Carole, Graeme & Marc Stewart)
Gerard, Carole, Graeme and Marc; if there is a prize for **excellence through innovation;** you should win it **every** time! Your undertaking has been massive, but so has your determination. You have created a world-leading product, congratulations; it has been a pleasure working with you.

www.weigh-ahead.co.uk

## THANKS

My thanks also go to the following people who in some way have helped me complete this book; you know the part you have played, so do I and I will never forget it. If I have accidentally missed someone, please feel free to write to me and say *'Hey John, you missed me out!'* and I'll include you in the next print run!

**Alphabetical order:**

**Arnaud de Beaumont**
A better friend no man could have. Thanks for your wisdom, support and wonderful humour over the years. Thanks too for the welcome you and Bénédicte always afford me. *À bientôt!*

**Sue Dowse**
Thanks for all the great help and support you've given me over the years Sue; it's been invaluable and is really appreciated.

**Dave Dunne**
Finally got the book out Dave! Thanks for your help over the years, much appreciated.

## Anna Gay

Thanks for your support and friendship Anna, you have been *amazing* over the book with some great advice. Thanks too for the opportunity to join you and Nick on occasions at NUFC, to eat hotdogs, drink beer and shout, *'Sit doon!'*

## Les Hodgson

Great working with you Les on many varied projects over the years; every client I know has valued your input.

## Ian Kings

I'm very grateful for the advice and help you gave me Ian.

## Ted Lenahan

To the best originator of truly ground-breaking products I ever had the privilege of working with. All the very best Ted to you, Maggie and Debbie.

## Jim Mackey

Thanks for your support over the years Jim and for making this book a possibility for me to complete; much appreciated.

## Dave McMenzie

Many thanks Dave for the time and assistance you've given me over the years; much appreciated!

## Newcastle University

Claire Adamson, Gareth Trainer, Jenny Biddulph and Rachel Murdie (hope I haven't missed anyone out?!). The *Elevator* is a very special place and the *enterprise vibe* you have created with your *Rise Up* programme, including *Rise up Pitch* is wonderful! Proud to be a part of it!

## Jane Nolan

Great to see you and Robert recently and look back on the wonderful projects you kindly invited me to work on with you both. You have done so much to help and also to *inspire* a great many start-up and small businesses over the years and I include myself in that number.

## Northumbria University

Graham Baty, Roger Candy, Steve Ball, Stephanie Macht - thanks to all of you (and the others in your team that I may have accidentally omitted). You all do so much good work in the field of enterprise; it's been a pleasure working with you and thanks for your support in allowing the *Stand-up Marketing* approach to lectures.

## Claire Riley

Thanks for *making it possible* Claire! I can't thank you enough for the time and support you have given me; without it this book wouldn't exist.

## Alex Shiel

Thanks for the IP advice you gave me Alex, it was very much appreciated.

## Tom Wilkinson

Couldn't have a list like this without saying just how much I have enjoyed working with you Tom on so many varied and fantastic projects over the years. Your enthusiasm, dedication and professionalism always made it a real pleasure!

## Barbara Young

Thanks B for your **great** encouragement, support (and nagging!) without which the book would never have got finished! Thanks also for *'nailing a jelly to a wall!'*